Non-Verbal Reasoning

The 11+
10-Minute Tests

For the CEM (Durham University) test

Ages
9-10

Practise • Prepare • Pass
Everything your child needs for 11+ success

How to use this book

This book is made up of 10-minute tests and puzzle pages.
There are answers and detailed explanations in the pull-out section at the back of the book.

10-Minute Tests

- There are 31 tests in this book, each containing 17 or 18 questions.

- Each test is designed to cover a good range of the question styles and topics that your child could come across in the non-verbal reasoning sections of their 11+ test.

- Your child should aim to score at least 15 in each 10-minute test.
  If they score less than this, use their results to work out the areas they need more practice on.

- If your child hasn't managed to finish the test in time, they need to work on increasing their speed, whereas if they have made a lot of mistakes, they need to work more carefully.

- Keep track of your child's scores using the progress chart on the inside back cover of the book.

Puzzle Pages

- There are 10 puzzle pages in this book, which are a great break from test-style questions.
  They encourage children to practise the same skills that they will need in the test, but in a fun way.

Published by CGP

Editors:
Joe Brazier, Liam Dyer, Alex Fairer, Ceara Hayden, Sharon Keeley-Holden, David Maliphant, Ben Train

With thanks to Alison Griffin and Rebecca Tate for the proofreading.

Please note that CGP is not associated with CEM or The University of Durham in any way.
This book does not include any official questions and it is not endorsed by CEM or The University of Durham.
CEM, Centre for Evaluation and Monitoring, Durham University and *The University of Durham*
are all trademarks of The University of Durham.

ISBN: 978 1 78294 628 1
Printed by Elanders Ltd, Newcastle upon Tyne
Clipart from Corel®

Based on the classic CGP style created by Richard Parsons.

Contents

These pages contain a completed example question for each question type that appears in this book. Have a look through them to familiarise yourself with the question types before you do the tests.

Odd One Out

Find the figure in each row that is most unlike the other figures.

Example:

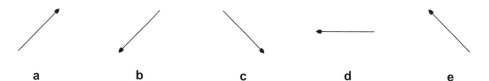

a   b   c   d   e

Answer: d

In all other figures, the arrow points diagonally.

Find the Figure Like the First Two or Three

Work out which option is most like the two or three figures on the left.

Example:

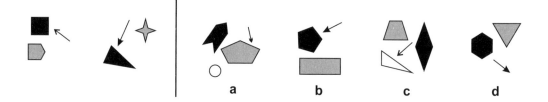

a   b   c   d

Answer: b

All figures must have an arrow pointing at a black shape.

Complete the Hexagonal Grid

Work out which of the options best fits in place of the missing hexagon in the grid.

Example:

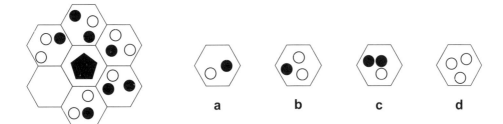

a   b   c   d

Answer: c

Going round the outer hexagons, the number of black circles alternates between one and two.

Complete the Square Grid

Work out which of the options best fits in place of the missing square in the grid.

Example:

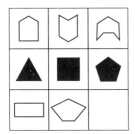

a   b   c   d

Answer: c

Working from left to right, the number of sides of the shape increases by one in each grid square.

Look at how the first two figures are changed, and then work out which option would look like the third figure if you changed it in the same way. (In some questions just one figure will change into another. This figure will look like a bug.)

Example:

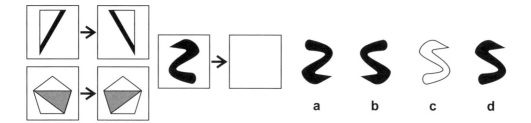

Answer: d

The figure reflects across.

Complete the Series

Work out which of the options best fits in place of the missing square in the series. (Occasionally, the series might be made up of two pairs of squares. These questions are solved in a similar way to Complete the Pair questions.)

Example:

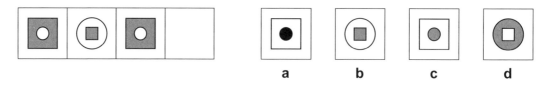

Answer: b

The figures alternate between a white circle in a grey square and a grey square in a white circle.

Rotate the Figure

Work out which option would look like the figure on the left if it was rotated.

Example:

 Rotate

                           a   **b**   **c**   **d**

Answer: d

The figure has been rotated 90 degrees clockwise.

Reflect the Figure

Work out which option would look like the figure on the left if it was reflected over the line.

Example:

 Reflect

                           a   **b**   **c**   **d**

Answer: b

Options A and D are rotations of the shape on the left. Option C has not been reflected.

Question Type Examples

3D Rotation

Work out which 3D figure in the grey box has been rotated to make the new 3D figure.

Example:

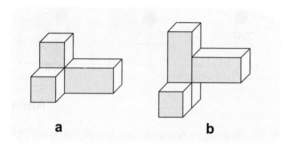

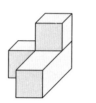

a

b

Answer: a

Figure A has been rotated 90 degrees right-to-left (see the glossary on page 142).

3D Building Blocks

Work out which set of blocks can be put together to make the 3D figure on the left.

Example:

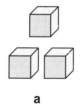

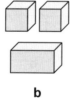

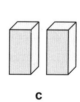

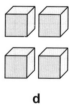

a   b   c   d

Answer: b

The block at the bottom of B rotates to become the block at the back of the figure. The two cubes move to the front.

Work out which option is a top-down 2D view of the 3D figure on the left.

Example:

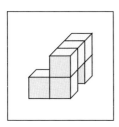 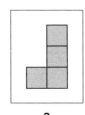 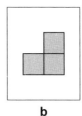 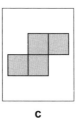 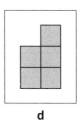

a   b   c   d

Answer: a

There are four blocks visible from above, which rules out options B and D.
There is a line of three blocks on the right-hand side of the shape, which rules out option C.

Cubes and Nets

Work out which of the four cubes can be made from the net.

Example:

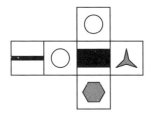

a   b   c   d

Answer: c

There is no black circle, which rules out option A. The thick black line and the thin black line must be on opposite sides, which rules out option B. There is only one grey hexagon, which rules out option D.

Test 1

You have **10 minutes** to do this test. Circle the letter for each correct answer.

Work out which option would look like the figure on the left if it was reflected over the line.

Reflect

1. |

                                      a   b   c   d

Reflect

2. |

                                        a   b   c   d

Reflect

3. |

                                        a   b   c   d

Reflect

4. |

                                        a   b   c   d

Reflect

5. |

                                        a   b   c   d

Find the figure in each row that is most unlike the others.

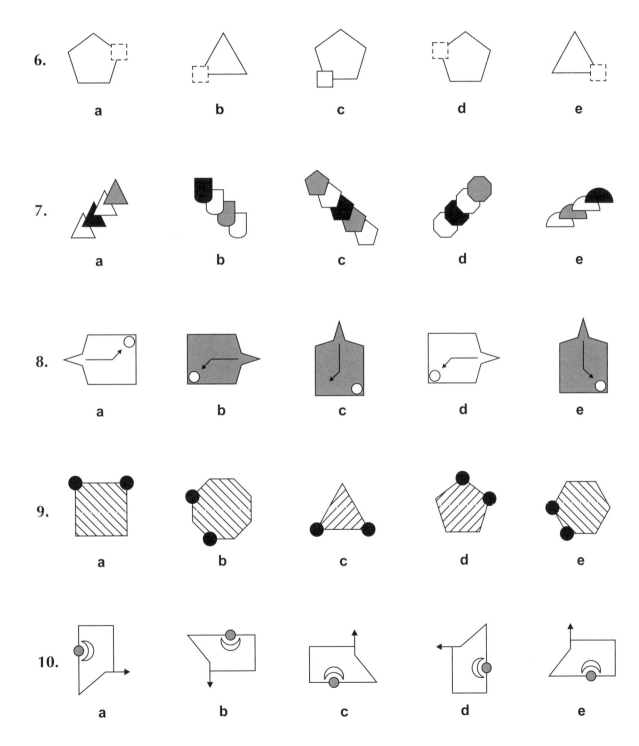

6. a b c d e

7. a b c d e

8. a b c d e

9. a b c d e

10. a b c d e

Test 1

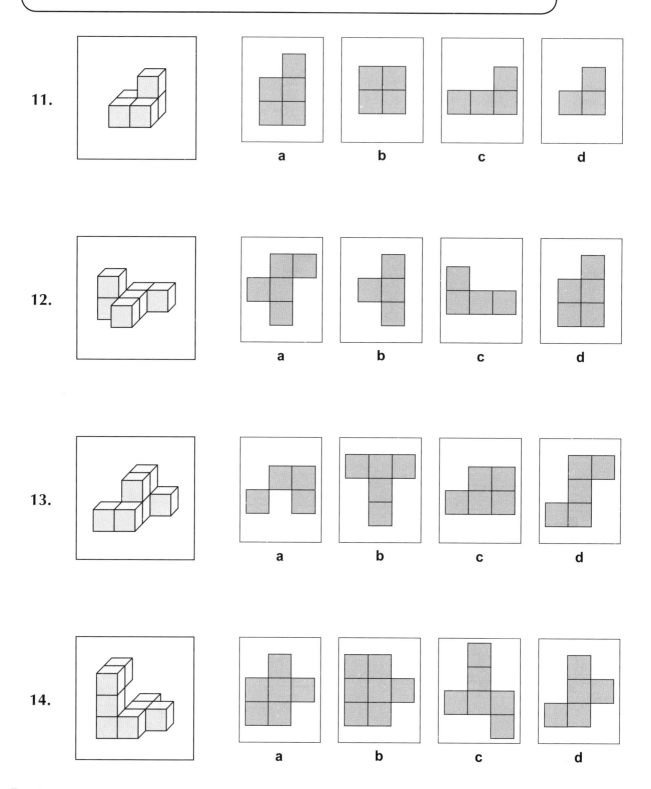

11.

a   b   c   d

12.

a   b   c   d

13.

a   b   c   d

14.

a   b   c   d

10

Work out which of the options best fits in place of the missing hexagon in the grid.

15.

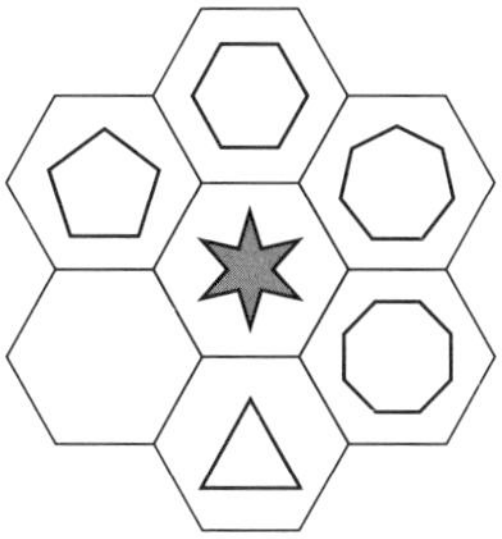

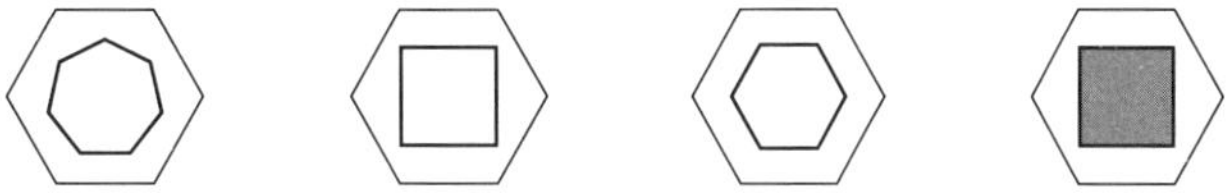

a b c d

16.

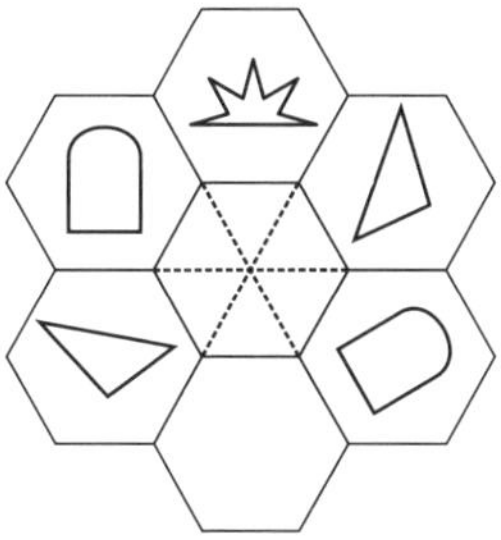

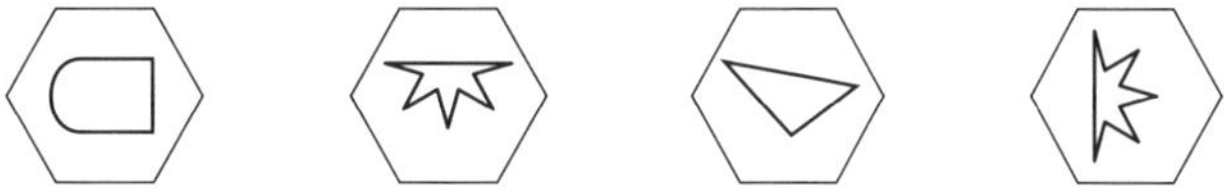

a b c d

17.

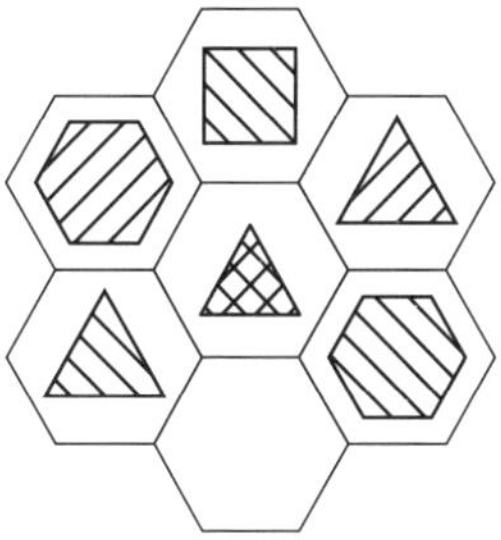

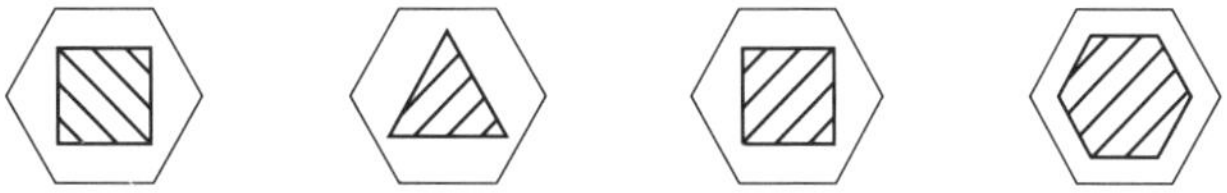

a b c d

18.

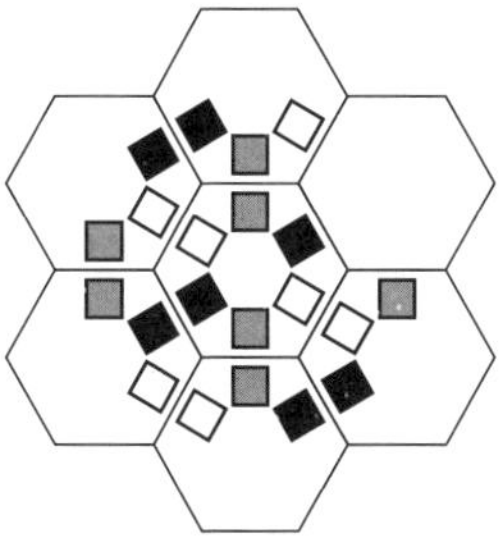

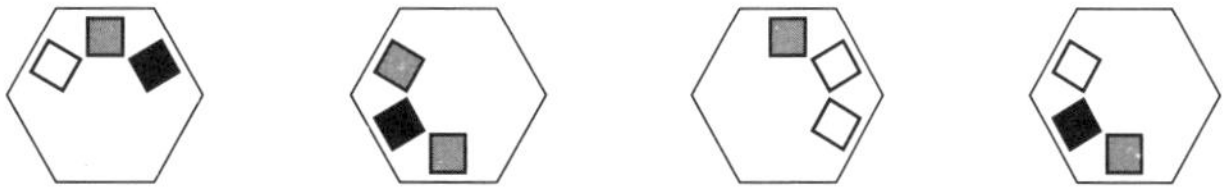

a b c d

/ 18

11

Test 2

You have **10 minutes** to do this test. Circle the letter for each correct answer.

Look at how the first two figures are changed, and then work out which option would look like the third figure if you changed it in the same way.

1.

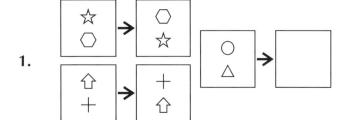
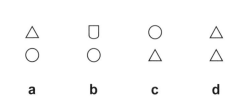

2.

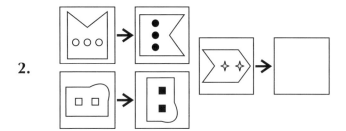
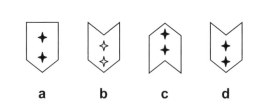

3.

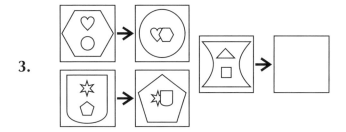
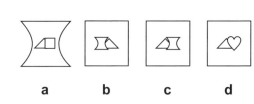

4.

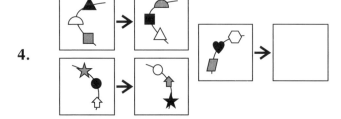
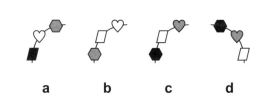

Test 2   12   © CGP — not to be photocopied

Work out which option would look like the figure on the left if it was rotated.

5. 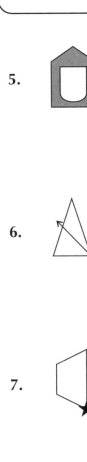 **Rotate**

              a   **b**   **c**   **d**

6. **Rotate**

              a   **b**   **c**   **d**

7. **Rotate**

              a   **b**   **c**   **d**

8. **Rotate**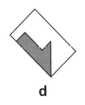

              a   **b**   **c**   **d**

9. **Rotate**

              a   **b**   **c**   **d**

Work out which of the four cubes can be made from the net.

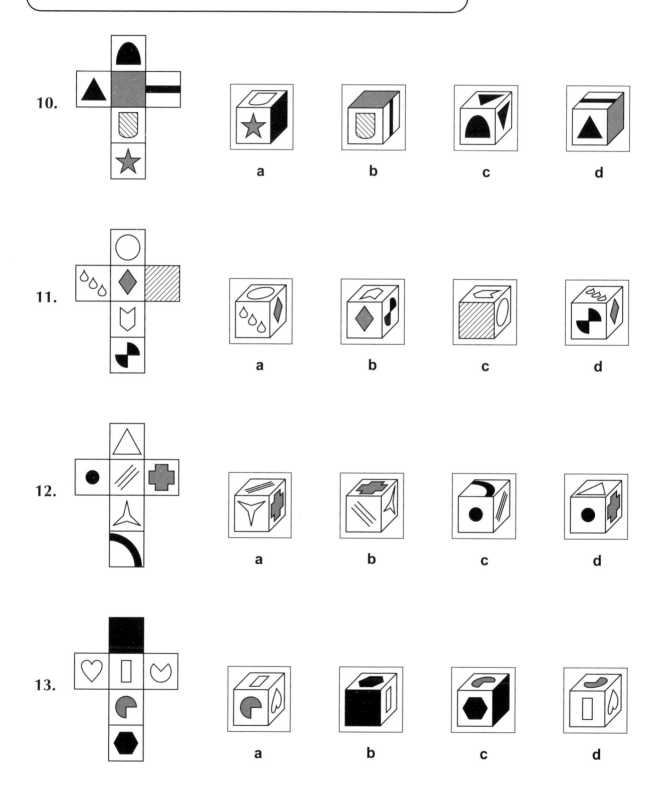

10. a   b   c   d

11. a   b   c   d

12. a   b   c   d

13. a   b   c   d

14

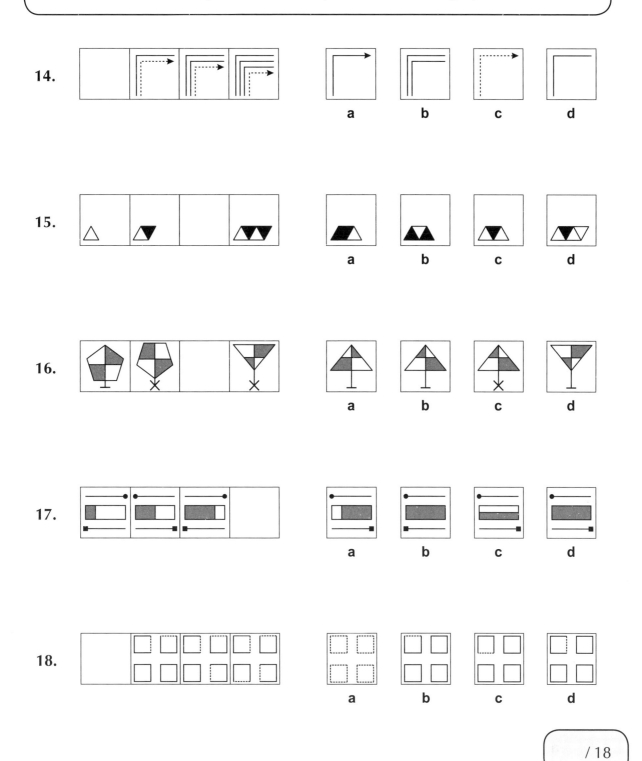

14.

a   b   c   d

15.

a   b   c   d

16.

a   b   c   d

17.

a   b   c   d

18.

a   b   c   d

/ 18

Test 3

You have **10 minutes** to do this test. Circle the letter for each correct answer.

Find the figure in each row that is most unlike the others.

1.

    a   **b**   **c**   **d**   **e**

2.

    a   **b**   **c**   **d**   **e**

3.

    a   **b**   **c**   **d**   **e**

4.

    a   **b**   **c**   **d**   **e**

Work out which of the four cubes can be made from the net.

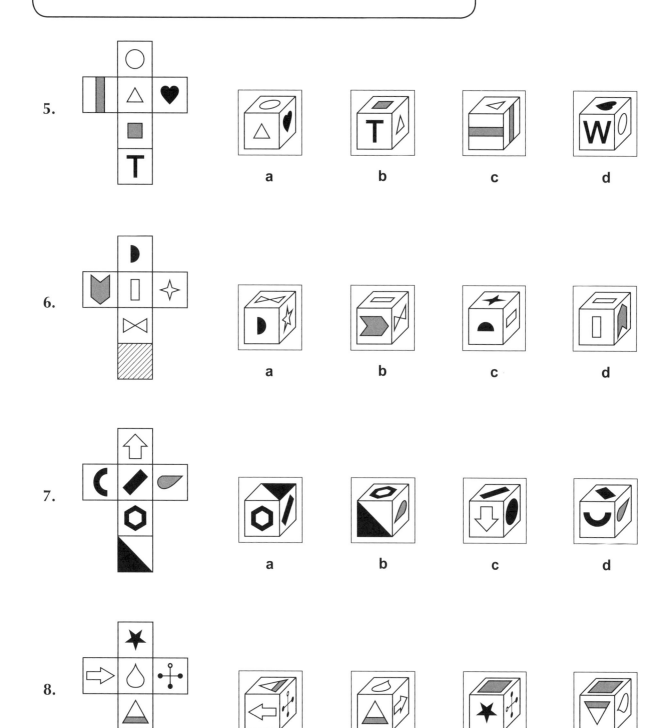

5.

a　　**b**　　**c**　　**d**

6.

a　　**b**　　**c**　　**d**

7.

a　　**b**　　**c**　　**d**

8.

a　　**b**　　**c**　　**d**

Look at how the first bug changes to become the second bug. Then work out which option would look like the third bug if you changed it in the same way.

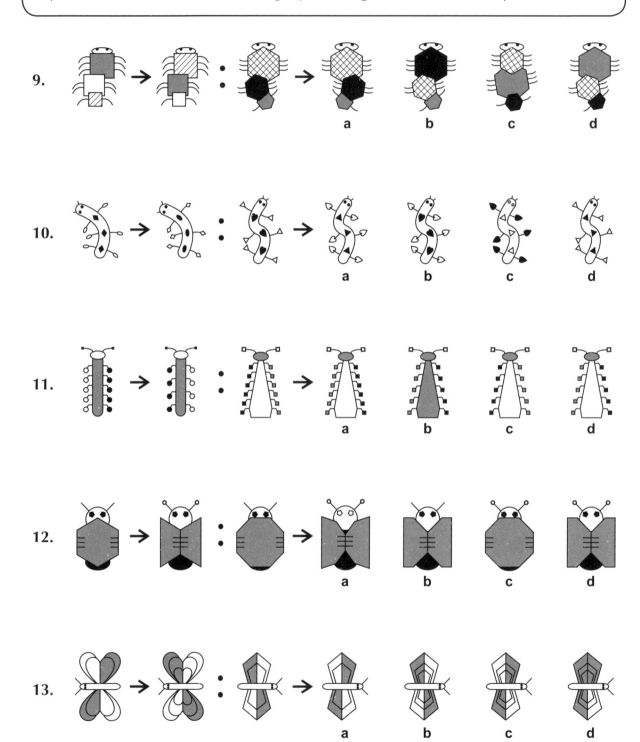

9.

a   b   c   d

10.

a   b   c   d

11.

a   b   c   d

12.

a   b   c   d

13.

a   b   c   d

18   © CGP — not to be photocopied

Work out which of the options best fits in place of the missing square in the grid.

14.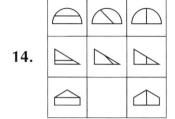

a   b   c   d   e

15.

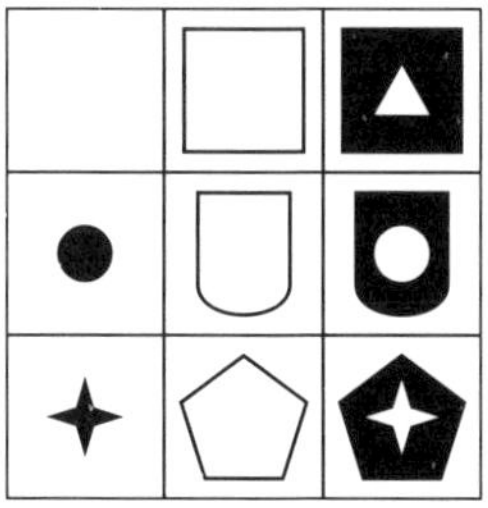

a   b   c   d   e

16.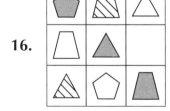

a   b   c   d   e

17.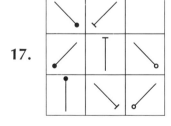

        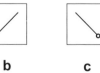

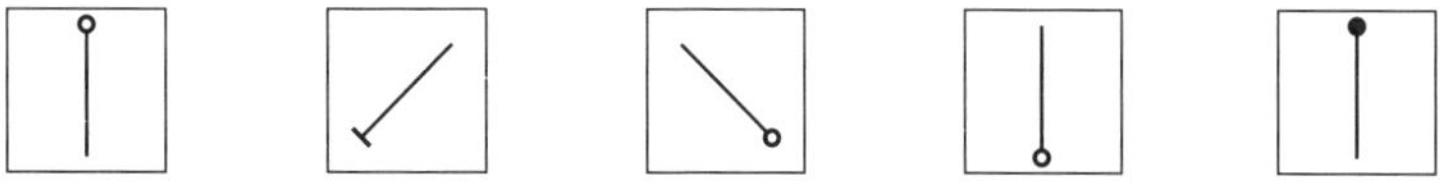

a   b   c   d   e

/ 17

Test 3

Puzzles 1

Time for a break! These puzzles are great for practising **nets** and **series**.

Stuck in the Mud

Chris is playing a computer game. He has to get the hare from the start to the finish by jumping on exactly five different cubes.

The top face of each cube can't be seen, and he will lose if the hare lands on top of a muddy puddle. He has a net to help him.

Draw the path Chris should make the hare take to get to the finish.

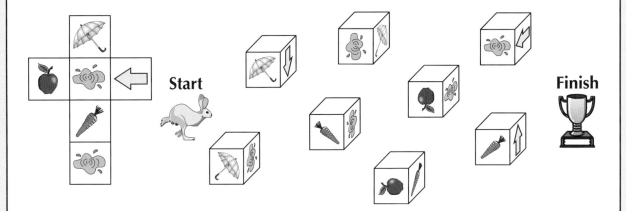

Soldiers on Parade

When a group of eight Roman soldiers stand on parade, they have to make sure that the patterns on their shields make a series. The first four soldiers are in place. Write the letters of the last four soldiers in the correct order.

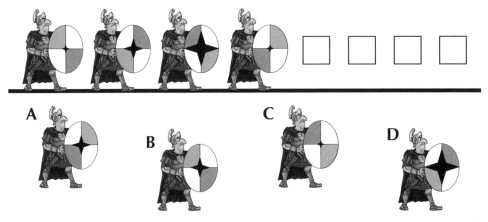

20

Test 4

You have **10 minutes** to do this test. Circle the letter for each correct answer.

Work out which of the options best fits in place of the missing square in the series.

1.

a **b** **c** **d**

2.

a **b** **c** **d**

3.

a **b** **c** **d**

4.

a **b** **c** **d**

5.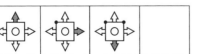

a **b** **c** **d**

Work out which of the options best fits in place of the missing square in the grid.

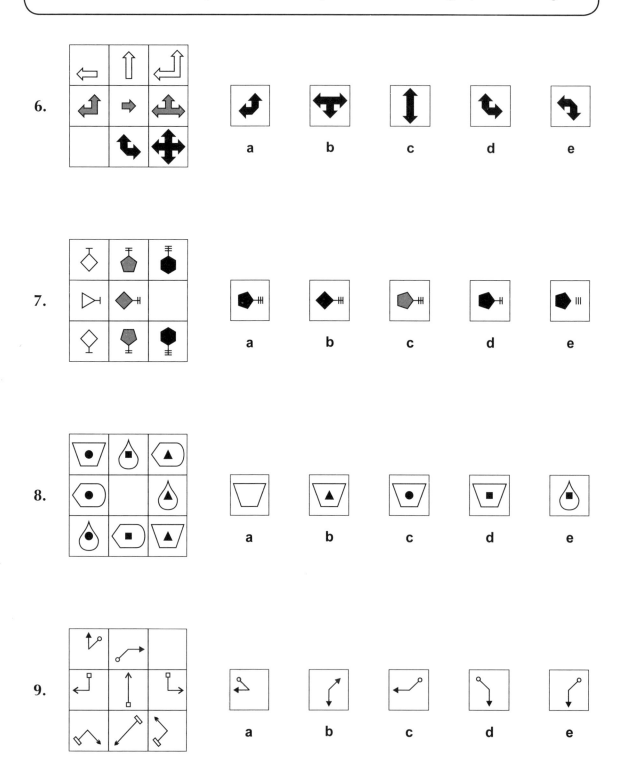

6.

a   b   c   d   e

7.

a   b   c   d   e

8.

a   b   c   d   e

9.

a   b   c   d   e

Work out which option is a top-down 2D view of the 3D figure on the left.

10.

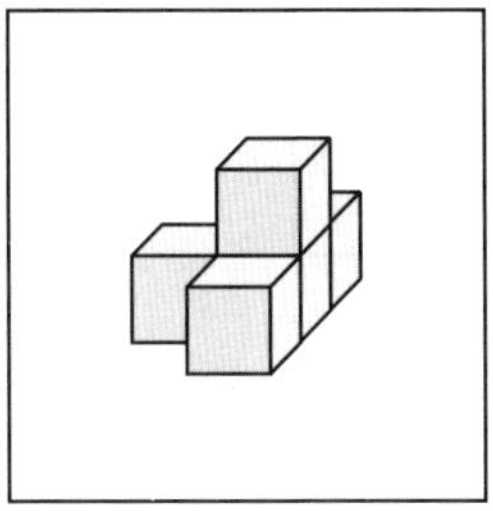

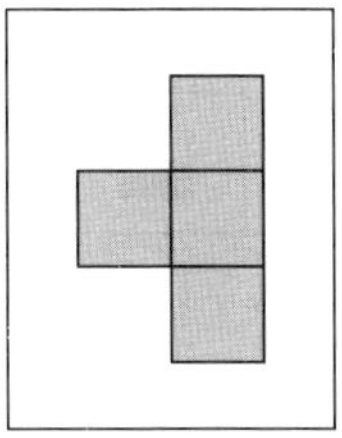

a 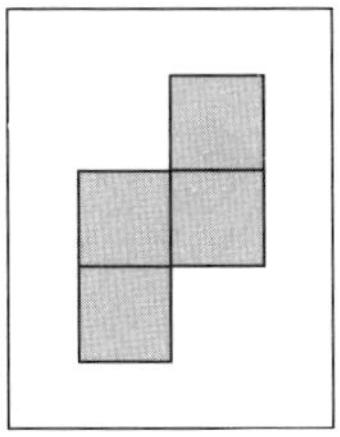   b 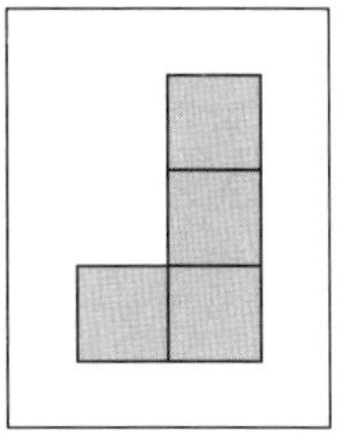   c 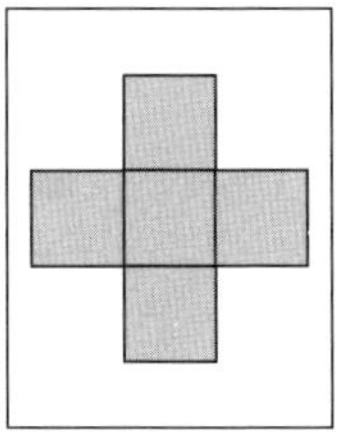   d

11.

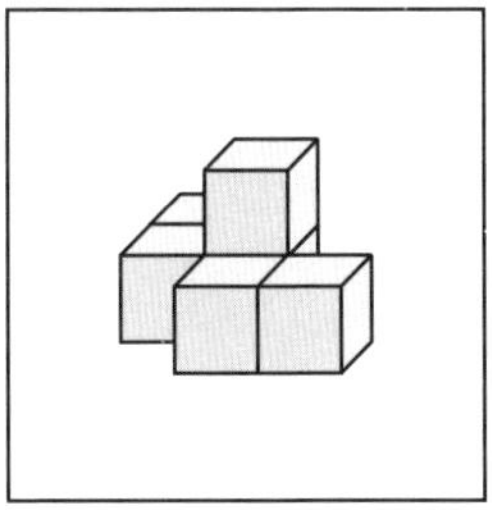

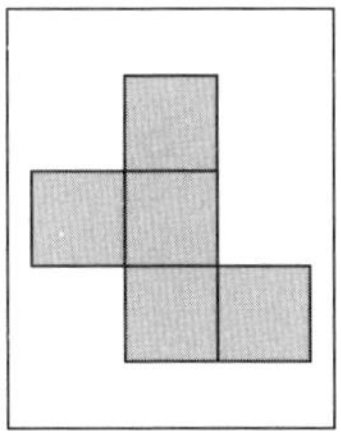

a 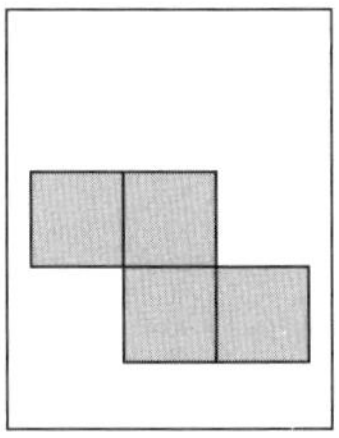   b 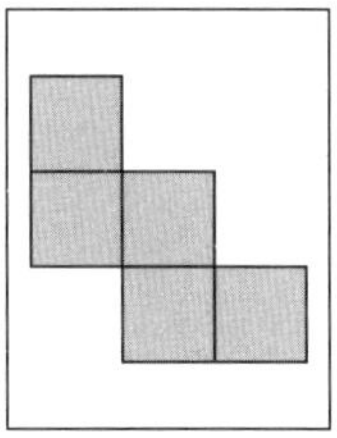   c 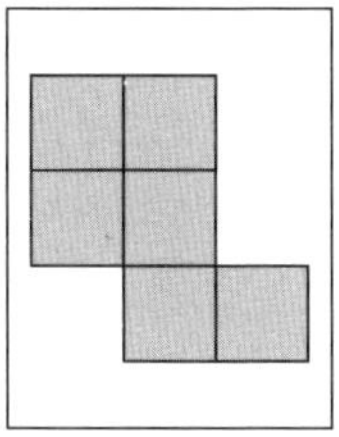   d

12.

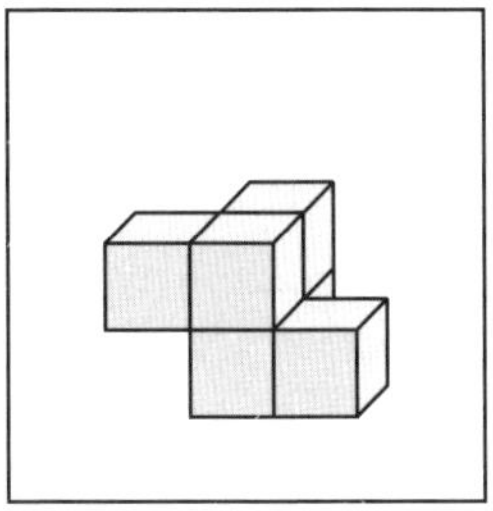

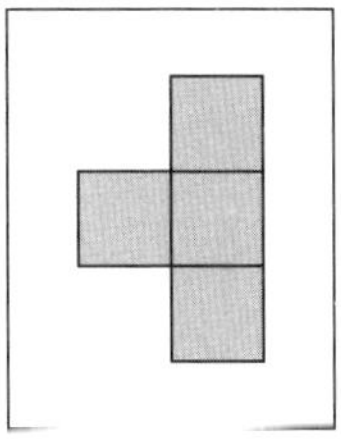

a 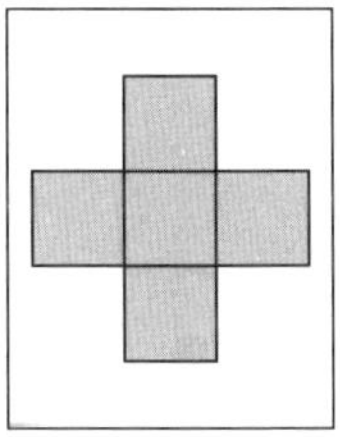   b 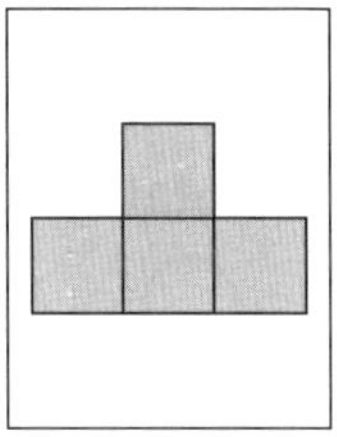   c 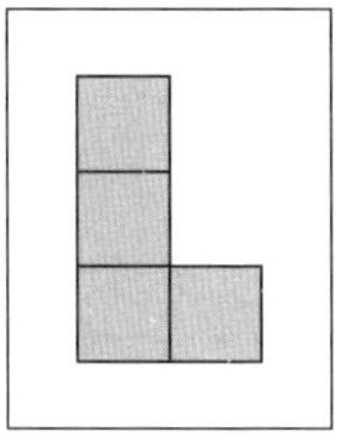   d

13.

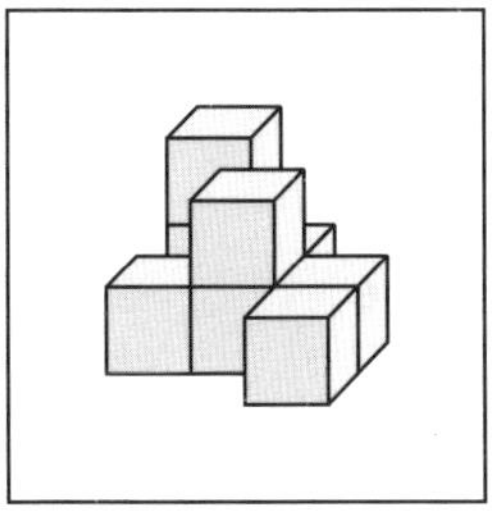

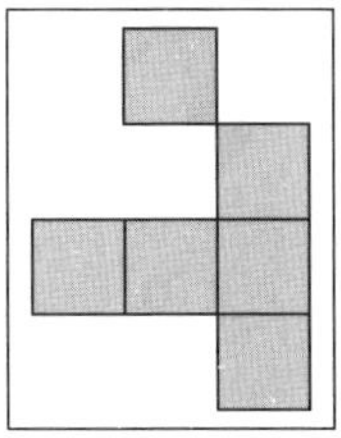

a 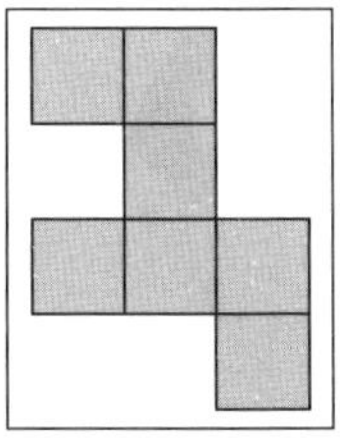   b 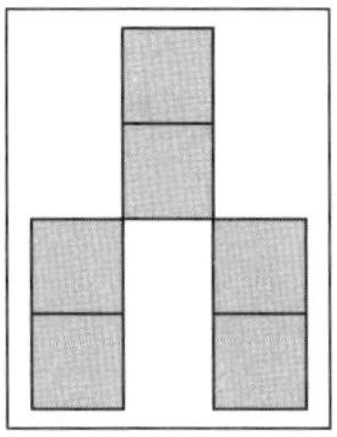   c 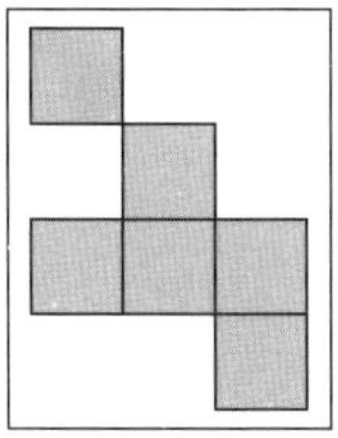   d

Work out which option would look like the figure on the left if it was rotated.

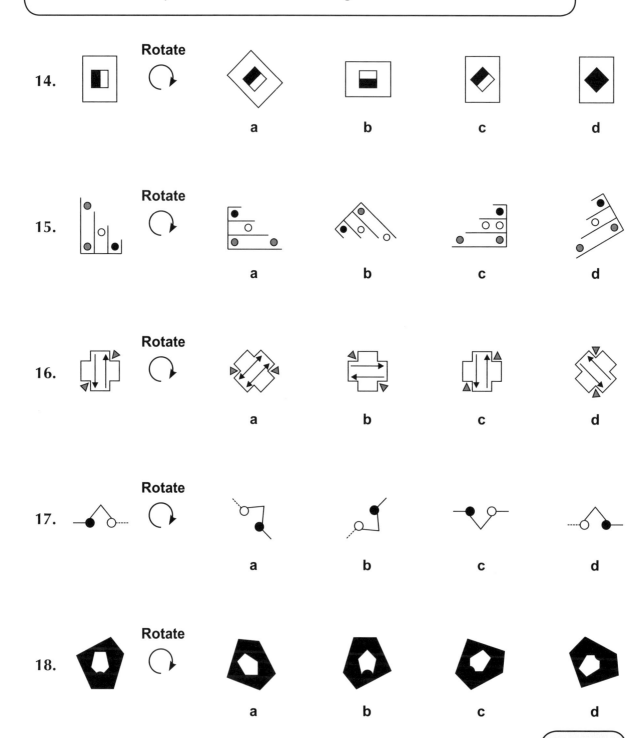

14.   Rotate   a   b   c   d

15.   Rotate   a   b   c   d

16.   Rotate   a   b   c   d

17.   Rotate   a   b   c   d

18.   Rotate   a   b   c   d

/ 18

You have **10 minutes** to do this test. Circle the letter for each correct answer.

Work out which option would look like the figure
on the left if it was reflected over the line.

Reflect

1.
 |

a   b   c   d

Reflect

2.
 |

a   b   c   d

Reflect

3.
 |

a   b   c   d

Reflect

4.
 |

a   b   c   d

Reflect

5.
 |

a   b   c   d

Test 5

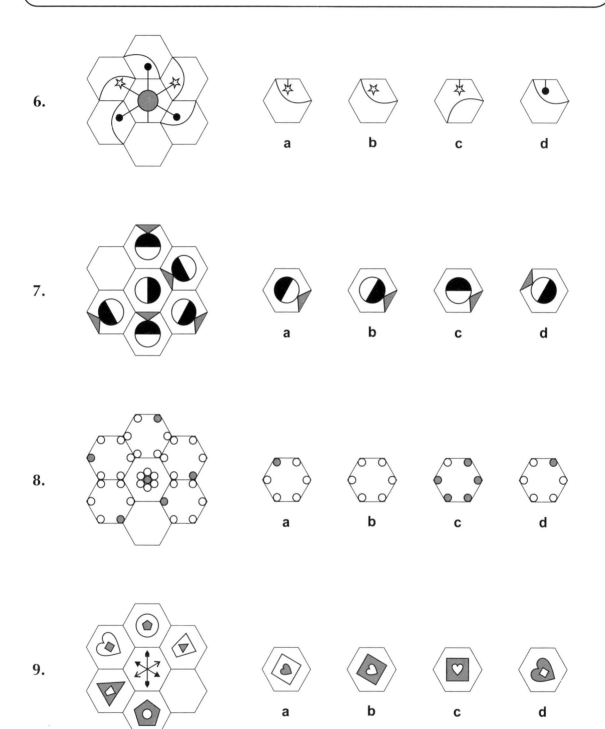

6.

   a   b   c   d

7.

   a   b   c   d

8.

   a   b   c   d

9.

   a   b   c   d

Work out which option is most like the two figures on the left.

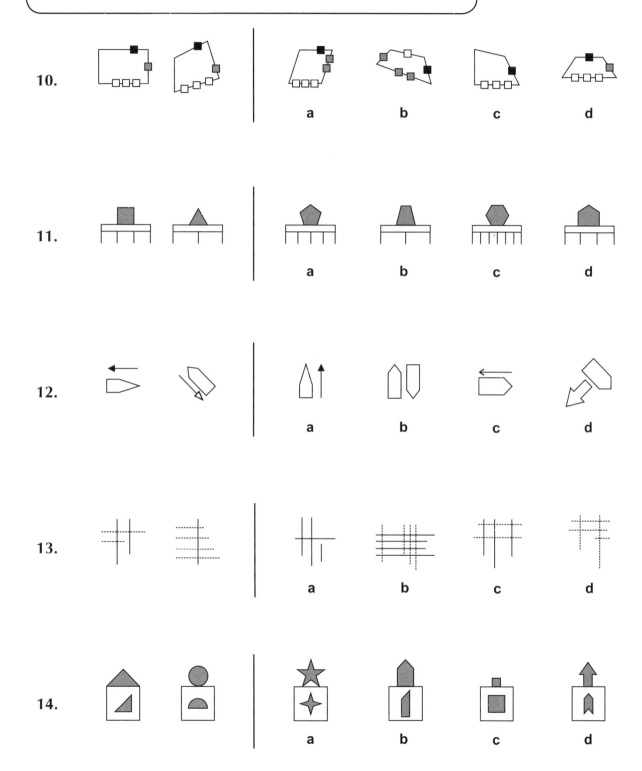

10.

a   b   c   d

11.

a   b   c   d

12.

a   b   c   d

13.

a   b   c   d

14.

a   b   c   d

© CGP — not to be photocopied   27   Test 5

Work out which 3D figure in the grey box has been rotated to make the new 3D figure.

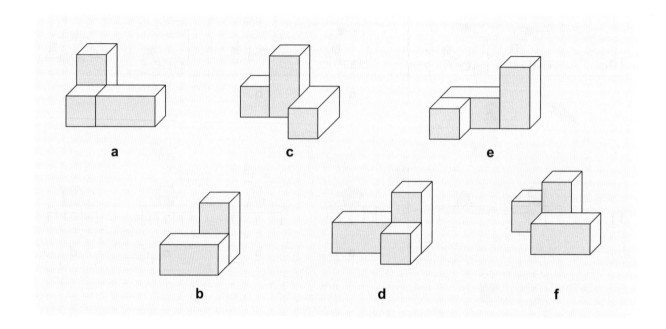

a   c   e

b   d   f

15.

a   d

b   e

c   f

16.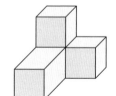

a   d

b   e

c   f

17.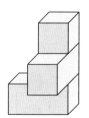

a   d

b   e

c   f

18.

a   d

b   e

c   f

/ 18

You have **10 minutes** to do this test. Circle the letter for each correct answer.

Work out which of the options best fits in place of the missing square in the grid.

1.

a

b

c

d

e

2.

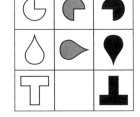

a

b

c

d

e

3.

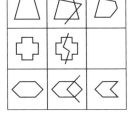

a

b

c

d

e

4.

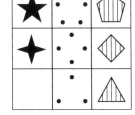

a

b

c

d

e

Look at how the first two figures are changed, and then work out which option would look like the third figure if you changed it in the same way.

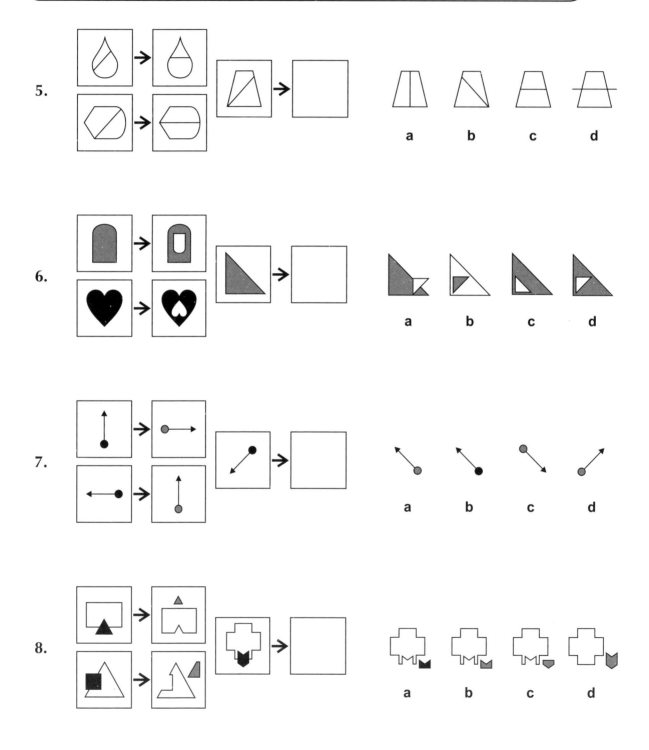

5.

a   b   c   d

6.

a   b   c   d

7.

a   b   c   d

8.

a   b   c   d

Work out which option is most like the three figures on the left.

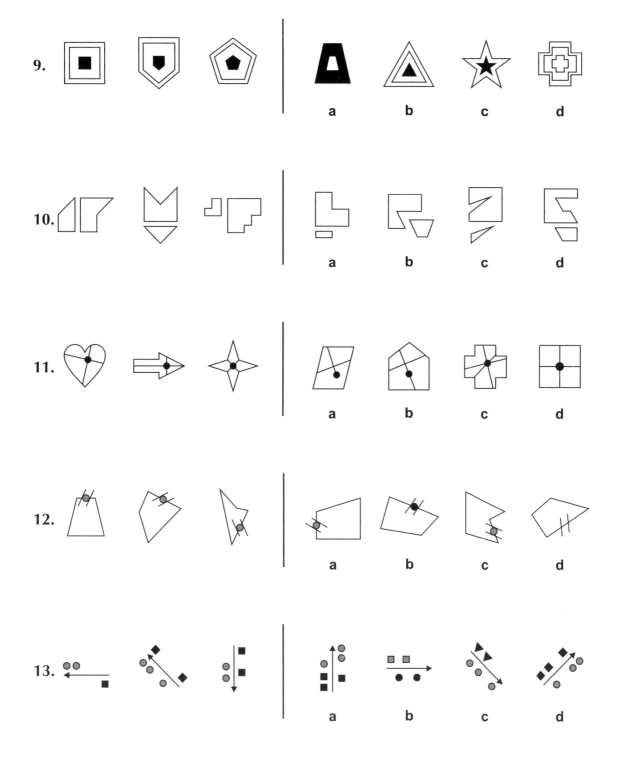

9.

    a   b   c   d

10.

    a   b   c   d

11.

    a   b   c   d

12.

    a   b   c   d

13.

    a   b   c   d

31

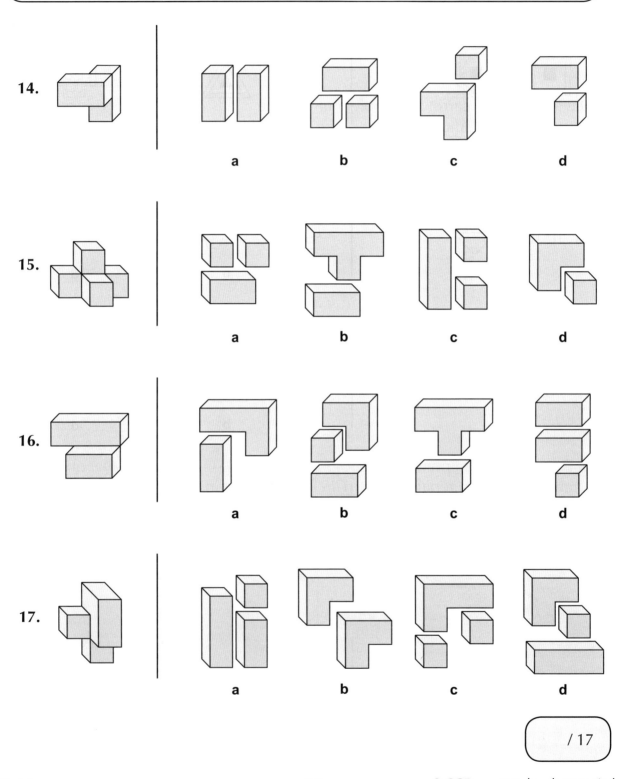

14.

a   b   c   d

15.

a   b   c   d

16.

a   b   c   d

17.

a   b   c   d

/ 17

Puzzles 2

These puzzles are perfect for practising your **pattern-spotting** skills.

A Recipe for Success

David is making carrot and apple muffins. He needs apples, carrots, eggs and flour to make the muffins. The grid below shows some of the steps that these ingredients go through. Label the right pictures with A-D to complete the grid.

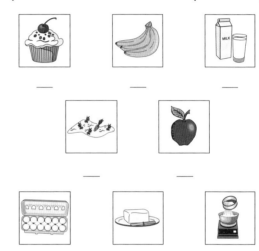

Pond Life

In Damon's garden pond, some frogs are sitting on some lily pads that are arranged in a hexagonal pattern. Circle which frog in the box below best fits on the empty lily pad.

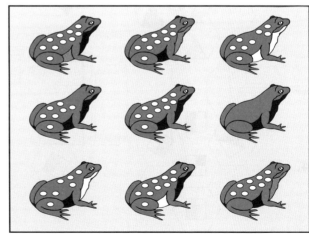

⏱ 10

You have **10 minutes** to do this test. Circle the letter for each correct answer.

Work out which of the options best fits in place of the missing hexagon in the grid.

1.

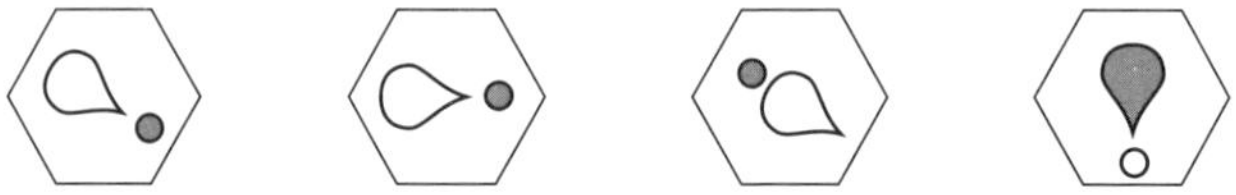

a   b   c   d

2.

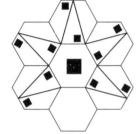

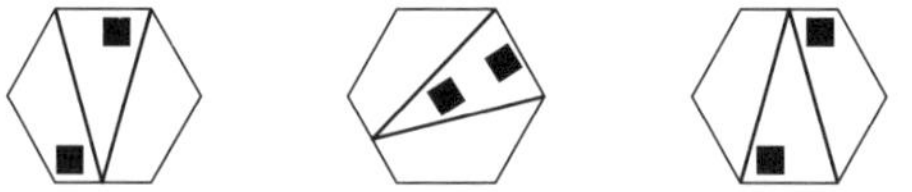

a   b   c   d

3.

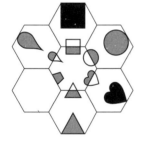

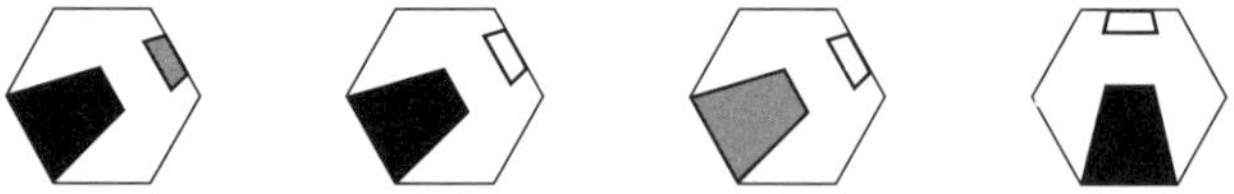

a   b   c   d

4.

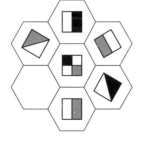

a   b   c   d

34

Work out which option would look like the figure on the left if it was rotated.

5. 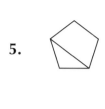 **Rotate**

                                                   a   b   c   d

6. **Rotate**

                                                   a   b   c   d

7. **Rotate**

                                                   a   b   c   d

8. **Rotate**

                                                   a   b   c   d

9. **Rotate**

                                                   a   b   c   d

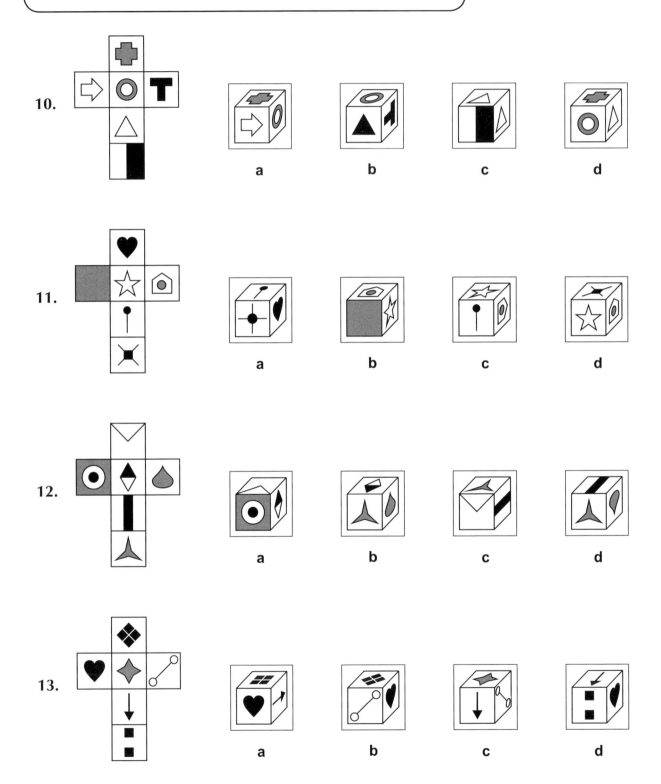

10.

a b c d

11.

a b c d

12.

a b c d

13.

a b c d

Find the figure in each row that is most unlike the others.

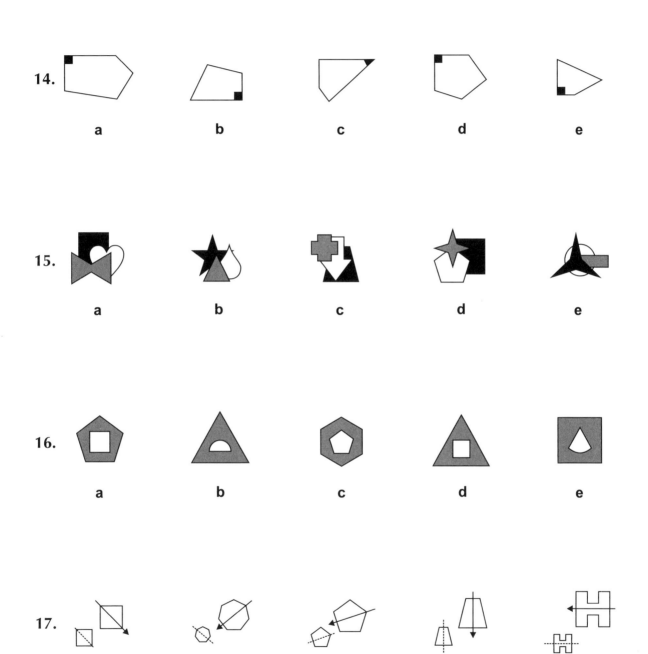

14. a   b   c   d   e

15. a   b   c   d   e

16. a   b   c   d   e

17. a   b   c   d   e

/ 17

37

You have **10 minutes** to do this test. Circle the letter for each correct answer.

Work out which set of blocks can be put together to make the 3D figure on the left.

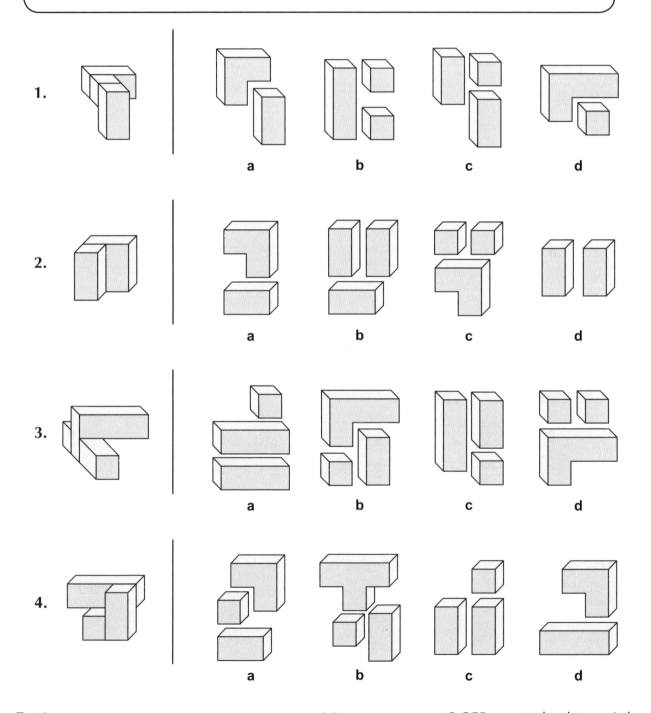

1.

a   b   c   d

2.

a   b   c   d

3.

a   b   c   d

4.

a   b   c   d

Look at how the first bug changes to become the second bug. Then work out which option would look like the third bug if you changed it in the same way.

5.

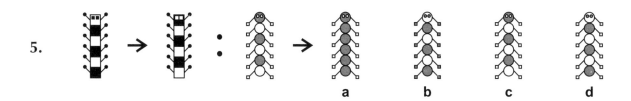

| a | b | c | d |

6.

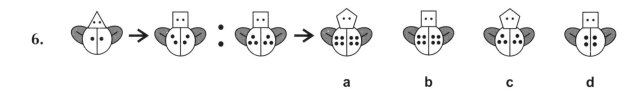

| a | b | c | d |

7.

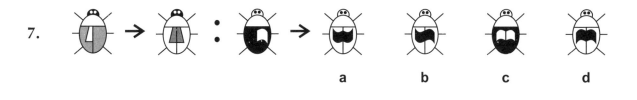

| a | b | c | d |

8.

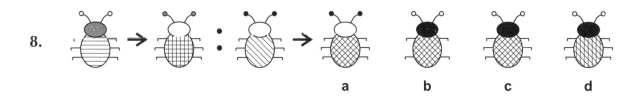

| a | b | c | d |

9.

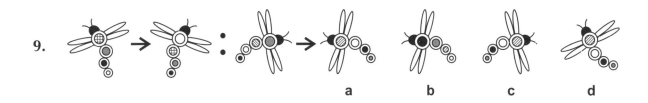

| a | b | c | d |

Work out which of the options best fits in place of the missing square in the grid.

10.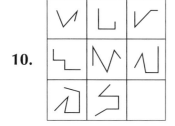

a

b

c

d

e

11.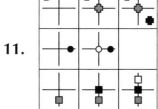

a

b

c

d

e

12.

a

b

c

d

e

13.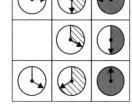

a

b

c

d

e

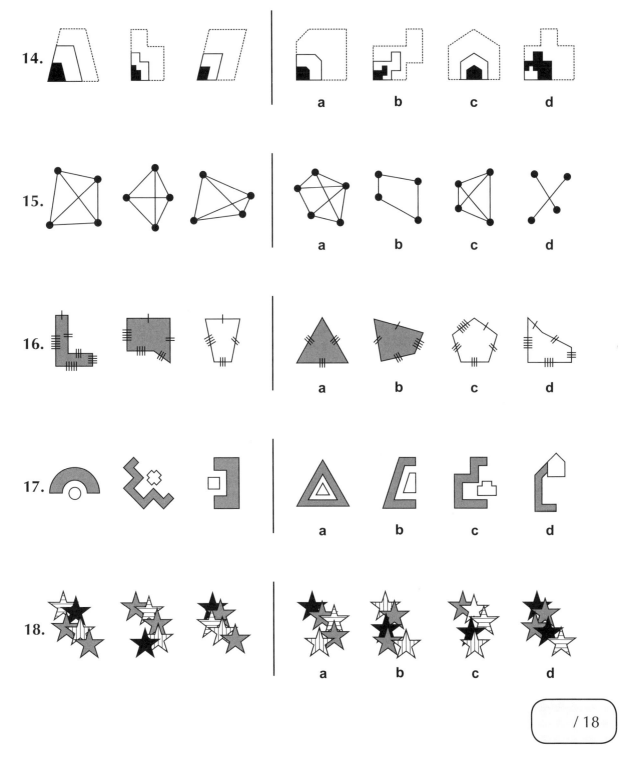

14.

a   b   c   d

15.

a   b   c   d

16.

a   b   c   d

17.

a   b   c   d

18.

a   b   c   d

/ 18

You have **10 minutes** to do this test. Circle the letter for each correct answer.

Work out which of the options best fits in place of the missing square in the series.

1.

                                                a   b   c   d

2.

                                                a   b   c   d

3.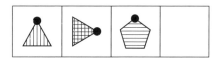

                                                a   b   c   d

4.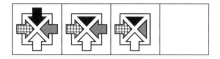

                                                a   b   c   d

5.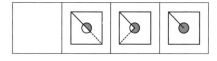

                                                a   b   c   d

Work out which set of blocks can be put together to make the 3D figure on the left.

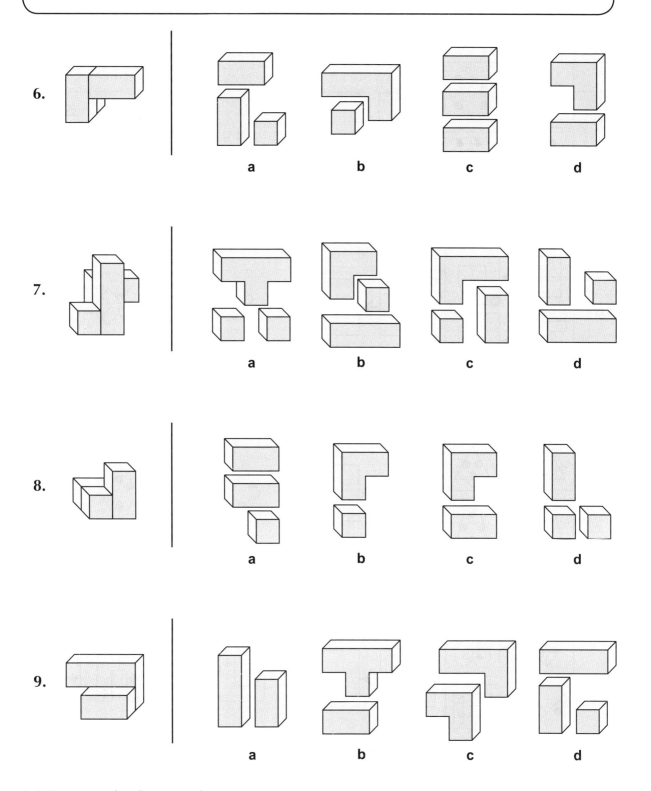

6.

a   b   c   d

7.

a   b   c   d

8.

a   b   c   d

9.

a   b   c   d

43

Look at how the first two figures are changed, and then work out which option would look like the third figure if you changed it in the same way.

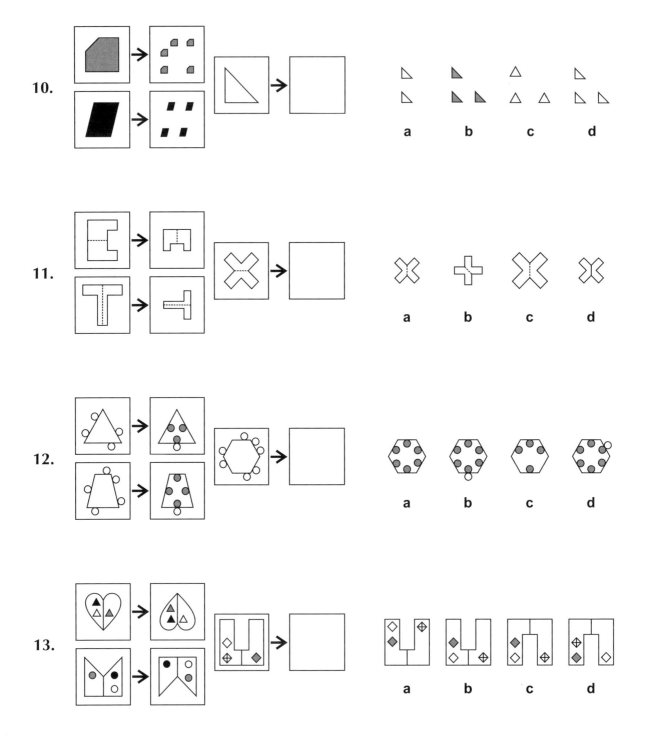

10.

a   b   c   d

11.

a   b   c   d

12.

a   b   c   d

13.

a   b   c   d

Work out which option would look like the figure on the left if it was rotated.

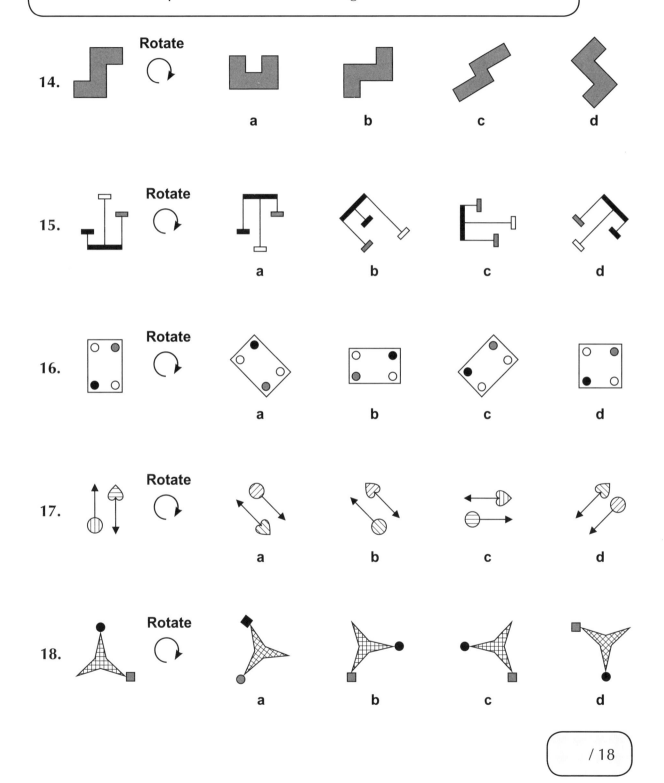

Get stuck into these puzzles — they're helpful for **reflecting** and **comparing** things.

Fake Photo Finish

Five photographs have been entered into a competition. Each photo must show reflection in water. The judge disqualifies four of the photos as the reflections aren't quite right, so the photos are fake. Circle the winning photo.

 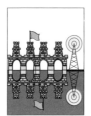   

Plane Spotting

A plane spotting guide shows the outlines of different types of aircraft. Choose the odd plane out on each page of the guide.

Test 10

You have **10 minutes** to do this test. Circle the letter for each correct answer.

Work out which of the options best fits in place of the missing square in the grid.

1.

    a   b   c   d   e

2.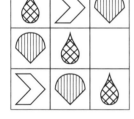

    a   b   c   d   e

3.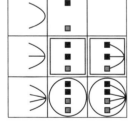

    a   b   c   d   e

4.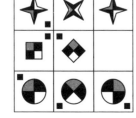

    a   b   c   d   e

Work out which option is a top-down 2D view of the 3D figure on the left.

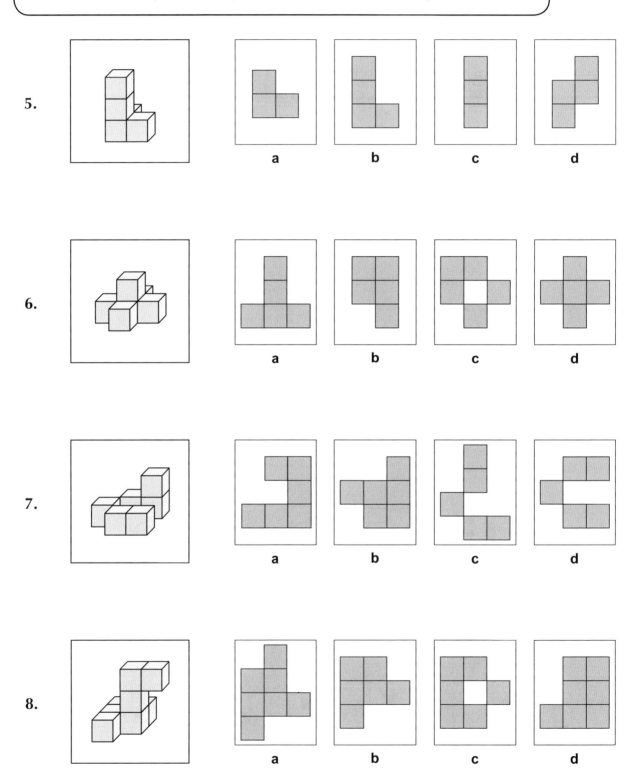

5.   a   b   c   d

6.   a   b   c   d

7.   a   b   c   d

8.   a   b   c   d

Work out which of the options best fits in place of the missing square in the series.

9.

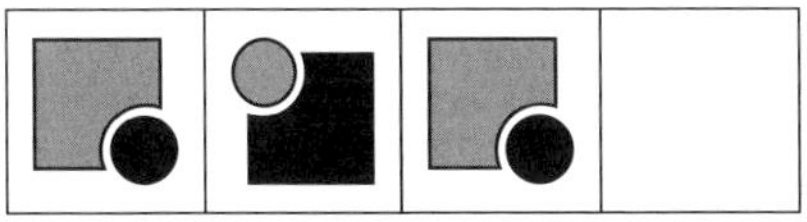

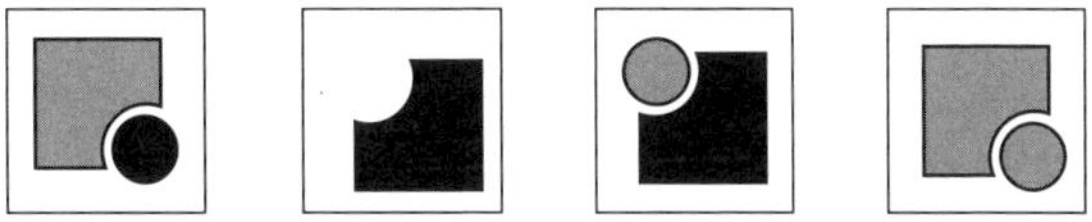

	a	b	c	d

10.

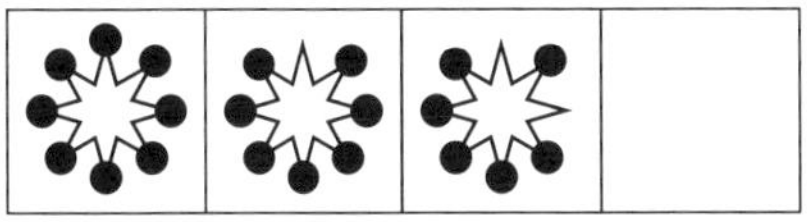

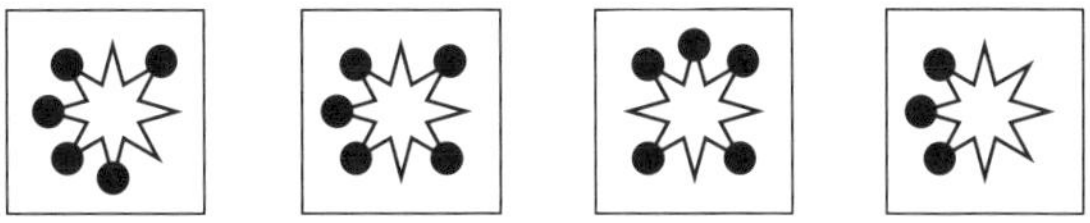

	a	b	c	d

11.

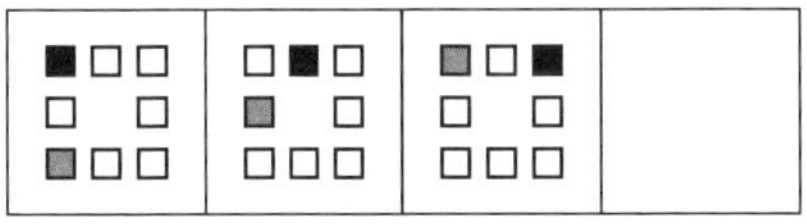

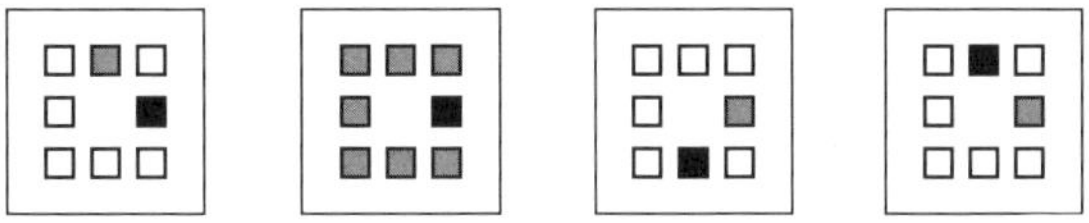

	a	b	c	d

12.

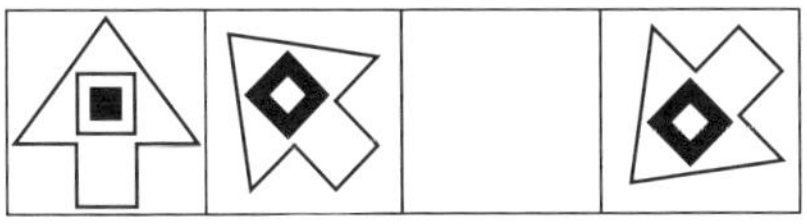

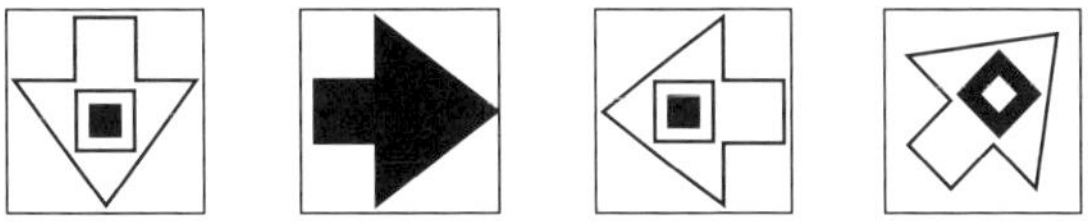

	a	b	c	d

13.

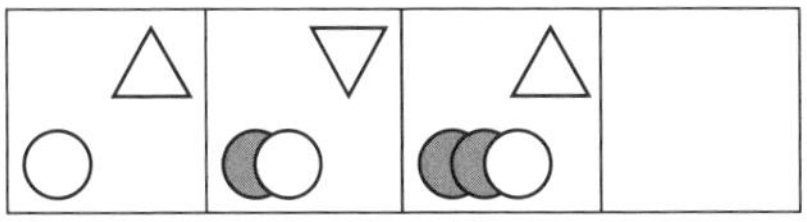

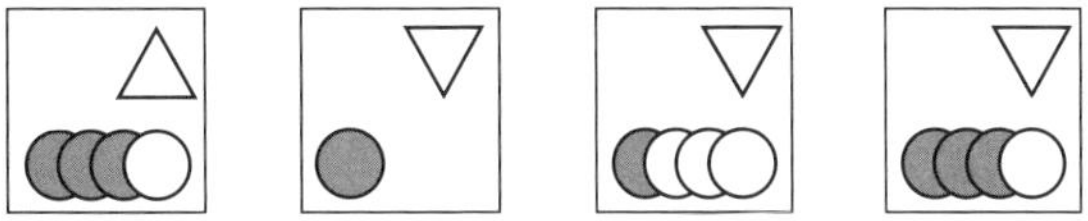

	a	b	c	d

Work out which option would look like the figure on the left if it was reflected over the line.

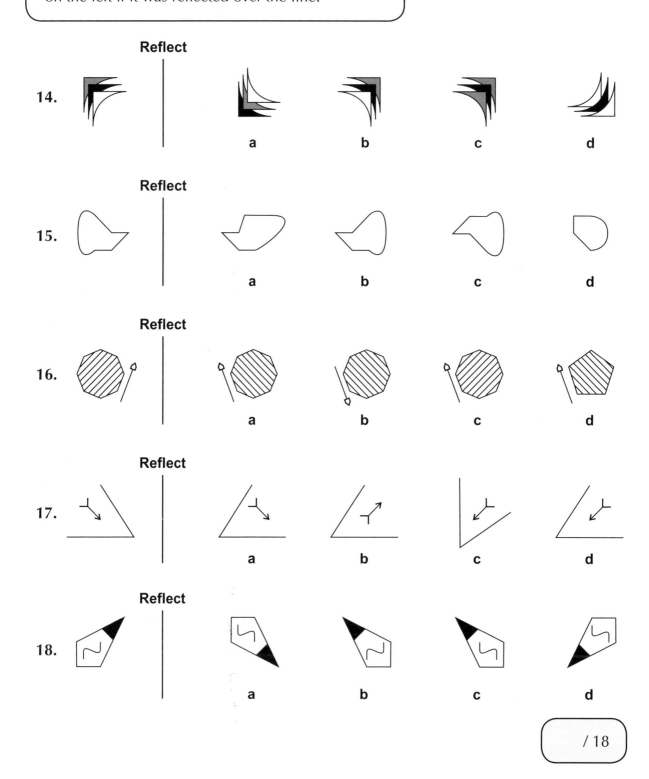

Reflect

14.

a　　　b　　　c　　　d

Reflect

15.

a　　　b　　　c　　　d

Reflect

16.

a　　　b　　　c　　　d

Reflect

17.

a　　　b　　　c　　　d

Reflect

18.

a　　　b　　　c　　　d

/ 18

Test 11

You have **10 minutes** to do this test. Circle the letter for each correct answer.

Work out which of the options best fits in place of the missing hexagon in the grid.

1.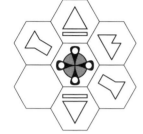

                                         a   **b**   **c**   **d**

2.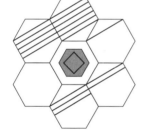

                                         a   **b**   **c**   **d**

3.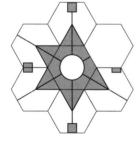

                                         a   **b**   **c**   **d**

4.

                                         a   **b**   **c**   **d**

      51

Work out which option is most like the three figures on the left.

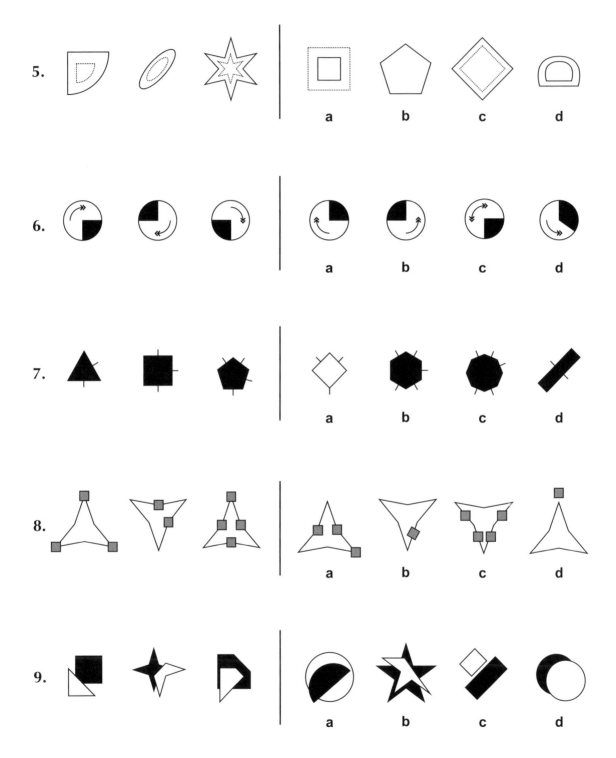

5.

     a   b   c   d

6.

     a   b   c   d

7.

     a   b   c   d

8.

     a   b   c   d

9.

     a   b   c   d

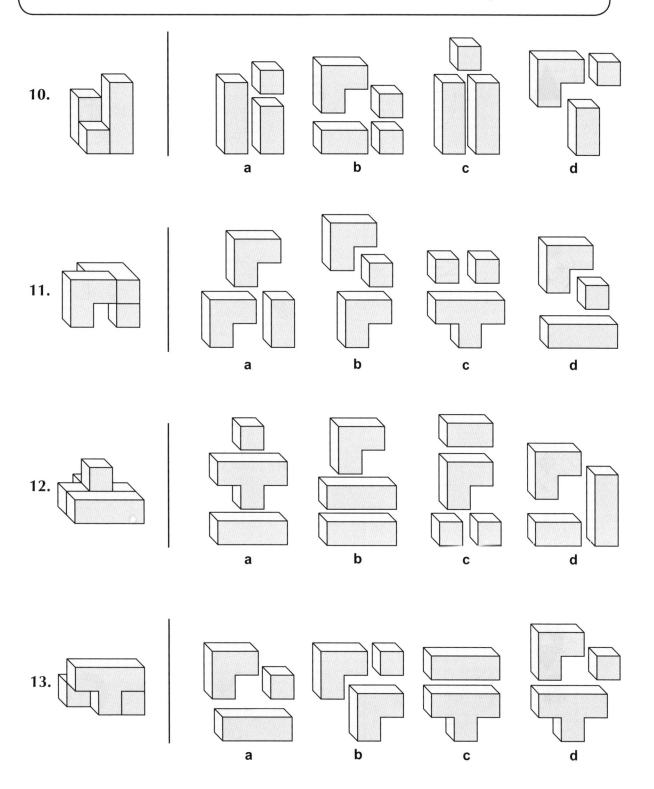

10.

a

b

c

d

11.

a

b

c

d

12.

a

b

c

d

13.

a

b

c

d

53

Find the figure in each row that is most unlike the others.

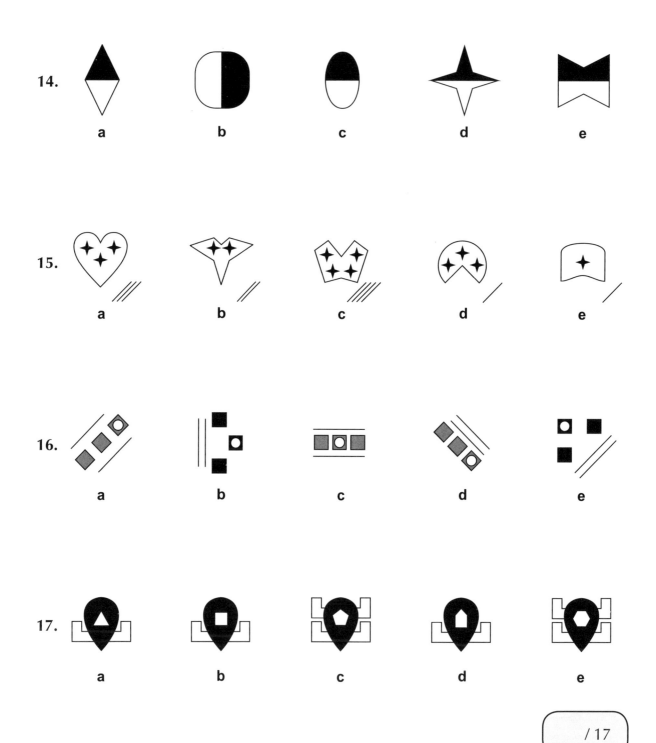

14. a   b   c   d   e

15. a   b   c   d   e

16. a   b   c   d   e

17. a   b   c   d   e

/ 17

Test 12

You have **10 minutes** to do this test. Circle the letter for each correct answer.

Work out which option is most like the two figures on the left.

1. |

                                       a   **b**   **c**   **d**

2. |

                                         a   **b**   **c**   **d**

3. |

                                         a   **b**   **c**   **d**

4. |

                                         a   **b**   **c**   **d**

5. |

                                         a   **b**   **c**   **d**

              Test 12

Work out which of the options best fits in place of the missing square in the series.

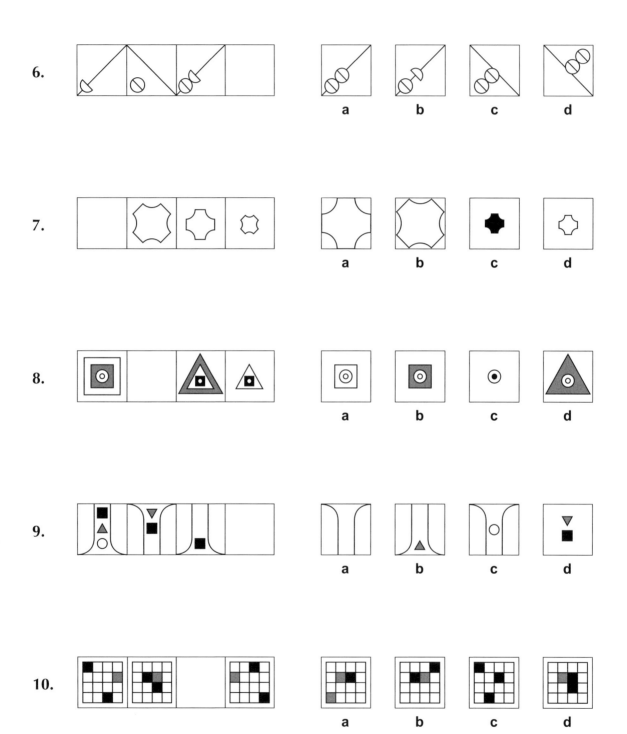

6.   a   b   c   d

7.   a   b   c   d

8.   a   b   c   d

9.   a   b   c   d

10.   a   b   c   d

Look at how the first two figures are changed, and then work out which option would look like the third figure if you changed it in the same way.

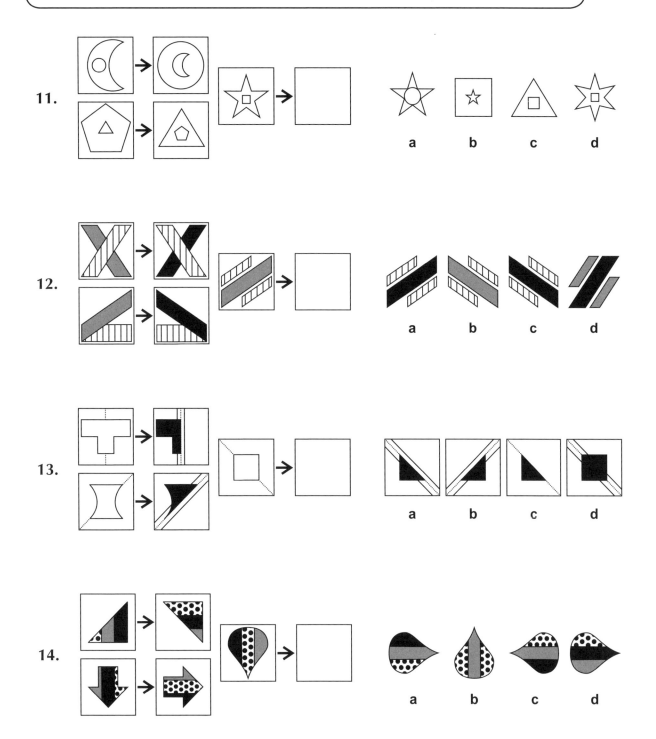

11.

a   b   c   d

12.

a   b   c   d

13.

a   b   c   d

14.

a   b   c   d

Work out which of the four cubes can be made from the net.

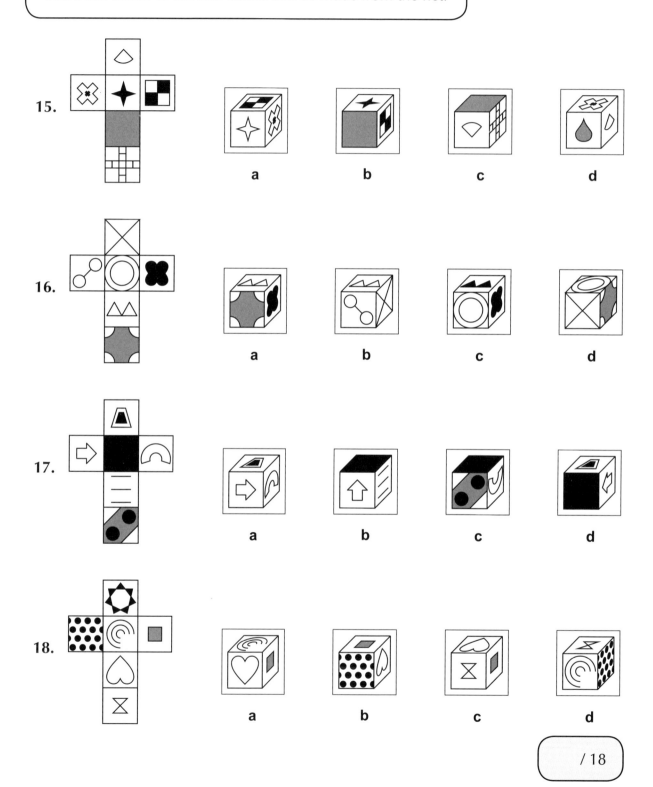

15.

      a   b   c   d

16.

      a   b   c   d

17.

      a   b   c   d

18.

      a   b   c   d

/ 18

Puzzles 4

Break time! Use your knowledge of **rotation** to work through the puzzles below.

Spinning Around

A spinner is shown on the right with six animals on it. It is spun twice and its new positions are shown below with most of the animals removed.

Draw a line from the right hippo to its correct place on each spinner.

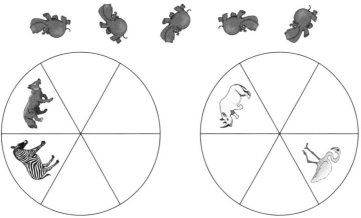

Monkey Puzzle

Micaela has made a monkey out of card. The card is grey on one side and white on the other. She draws all the parts on the card below before cutting them out.

Circle the monkey that she can make with her pieces of card.

Test 13

You have **10 minutes** to do this test. Circle the letter for each correct answer.

Work out which option would look like the figure on the left if it was rotated.

1. **Rotate**

                                       a   **b**   **c**   **d**

2. **Rotate**

                                       a   **b**   **c**   **d**

3. **Rotate**

                                       a   **b**   **c**   **d**

4. **Rotate**

                                       a   **b**   **c**   **d**

5. **Rotate**

                                       a   **b**   **c**   **d**

Find the figure in each row that is most unlike the others.

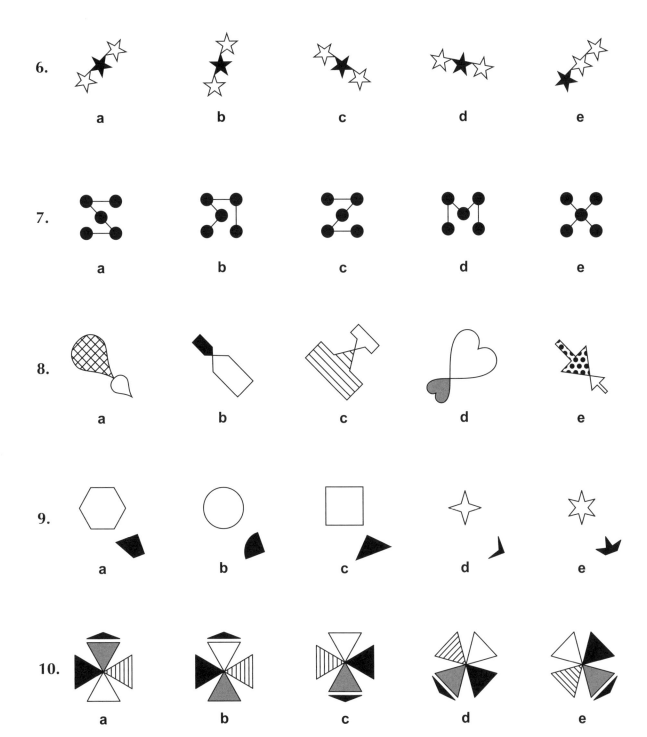

6.   a   b   c   d   e

7.   a   b   c   d   e

8.   a   b   c   d   e

9.   a   b   c   d   e

10.   a   b   c   d   e

Test 13

Work out which of the options best fits in place of the missing hexagon in the grid.

11.

a   b   c   d

12.

a   b   c   d

13.

a   b   c   d

14.

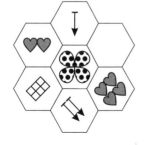

a   b   c   d

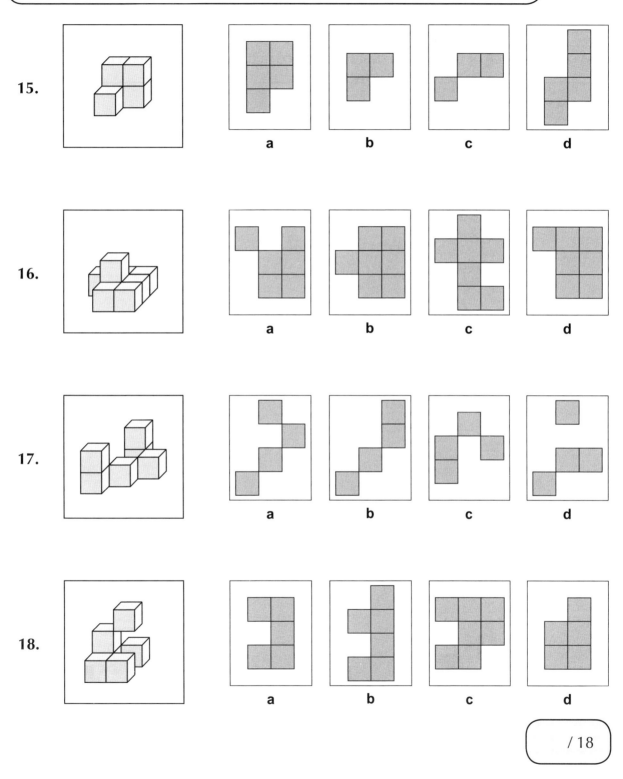

15.

a　　　　b　　　　c　　　　d

16.

a　　　　b　　　　c　　　　d

17.

a　　　　b　　　　c　　　　d

18.

a　　　　b　　　　c　　　　d

/ 18

Test 14

⏱ 10

You have **10 minutes** to do this test. Circle the letter for each correct answer.

Work out which of the options best fits in place of the missing hexagon in the grid.

1.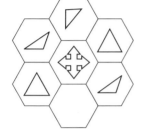

  a b c d

2.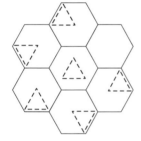

  a b c d

3.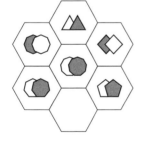

  a b c d

4.

  a b c d

64

Look at how the first two figures are changed, and then work out which option would look like the third figure if you changed it in the same way.

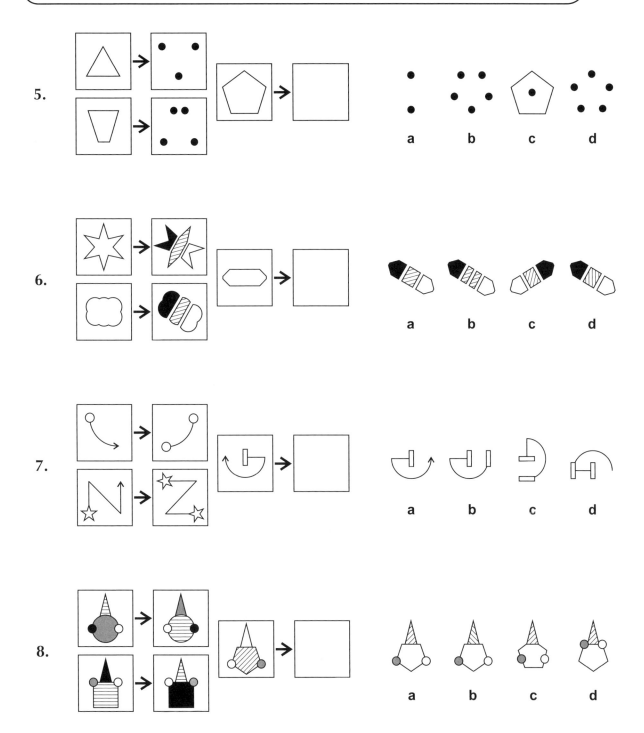

5.

a   b   c   d

6.

a   b   c   d

7.

a   b   c   d

8.

a   b   c   d

Work out which 3D figure in the grey box has been rotated to make the new 3D figure.

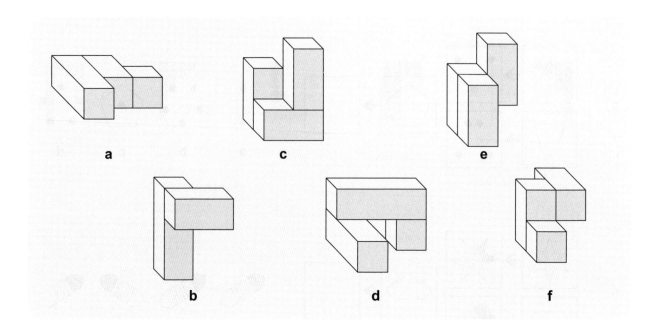

a   c   e

b   d   f

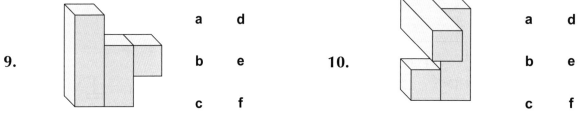

9.

a   d

b   e

c   f

10.

a   d

b   e

c   f

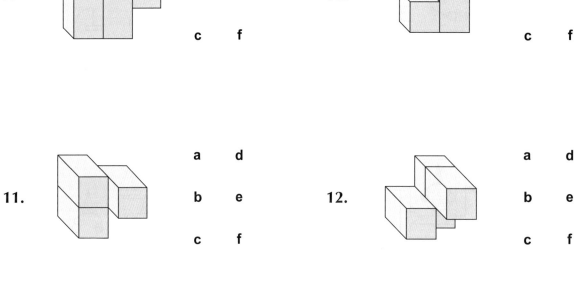

11.

a   d

b   e

c   f

12.

a   d

b   e

c   f

Work out which option would look like the figure on the left if it was reflected over the line.

Reflect

13.

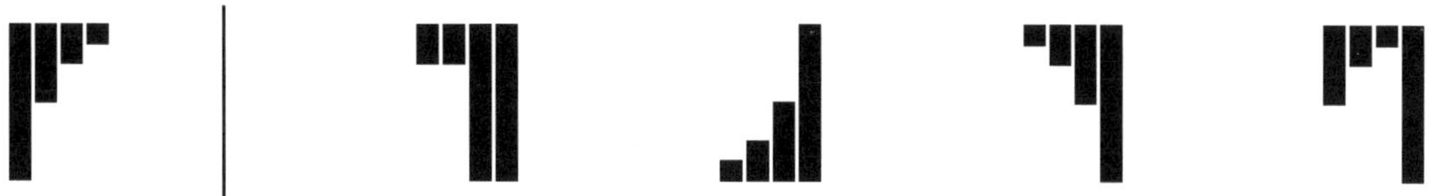

    a   b   c   d

Reflect

14.

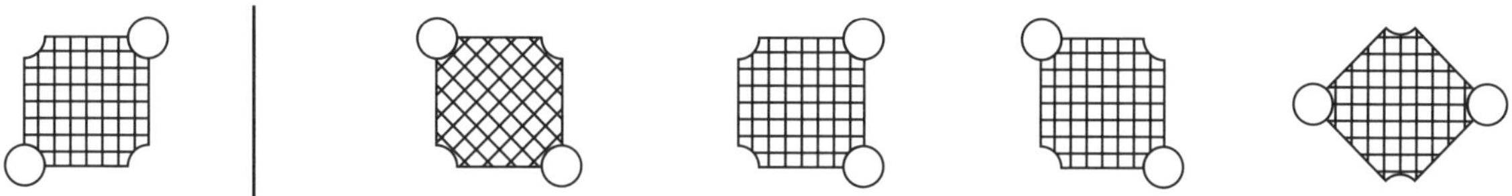

    a   b   c   d

Reflect

15.

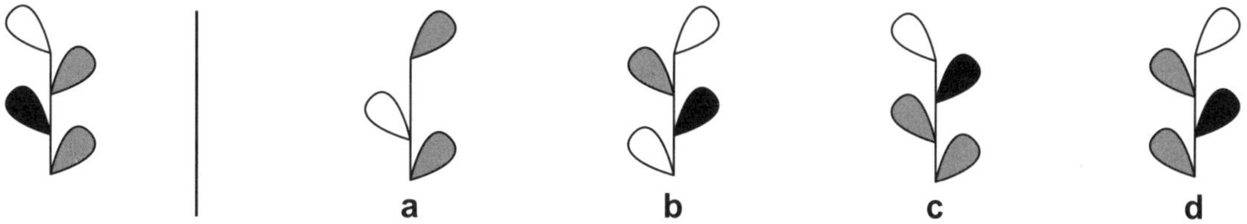

    a   b   c   d

Reflect

16.

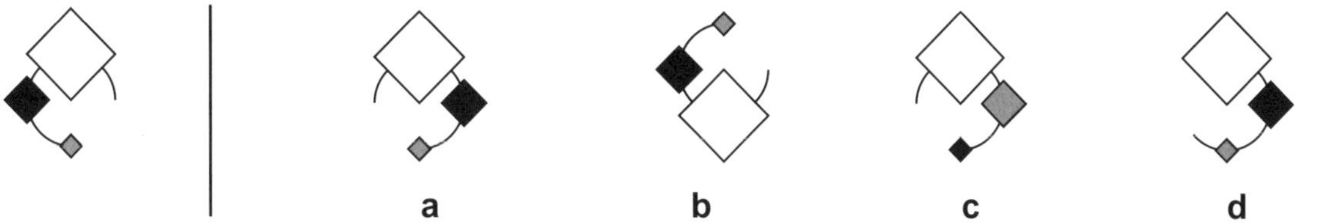

    a   b   c   d

Reflect

17.

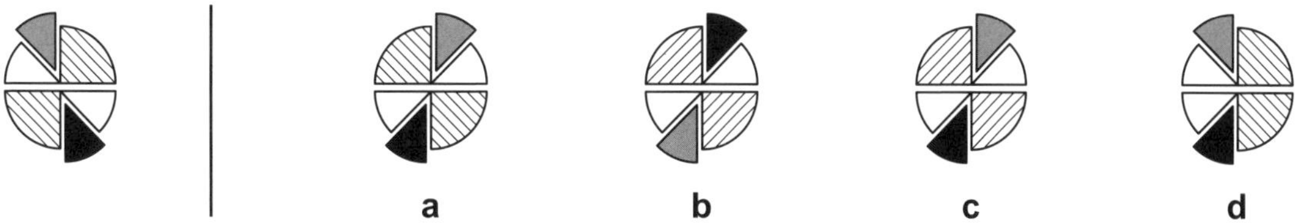

    a   b   c   d

/ 17

Test 14

Test 15

You have **10 minutes** to do this test. Circle the letter for each correct answer.

Work out which option is most like the two figures on the left.

1. |

                                               a   b   c   d

2. |

                                               a   b   c   d

3. |

                                               a   b   c   d

4. |

                                               a   b   c   d

5. |

                                               a   b   c   d

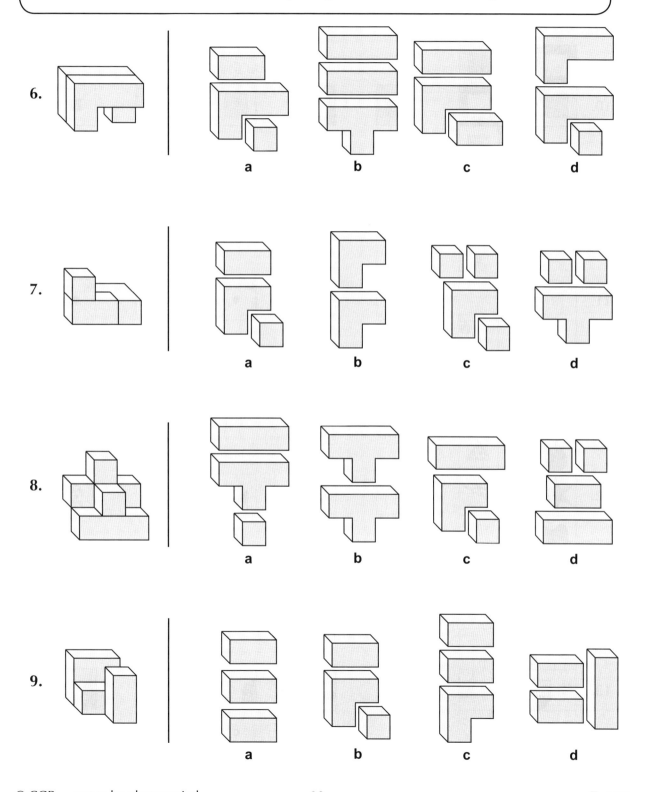

6.

    a   b   c   d

7.

    a   b   c   d

8.

    a   b   c   d

9.

    a   b   c   d

Work out which of the options best fits in place of the missing square in the grid.

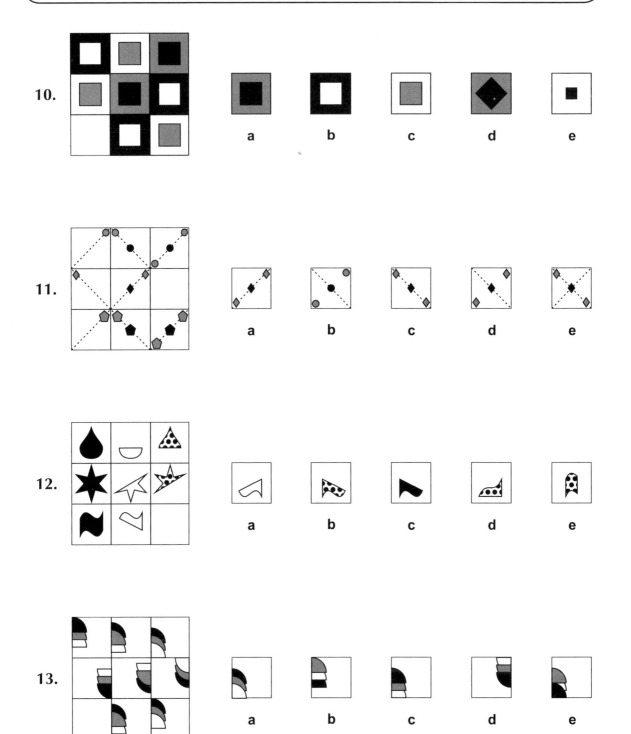

10.

a   b   c   d   e

11.

a   b   c   d   e

12.

a   b   c   d   e

13.

a   b   c   d   e

Work out which of the options best fits in place of the missing square in the series.

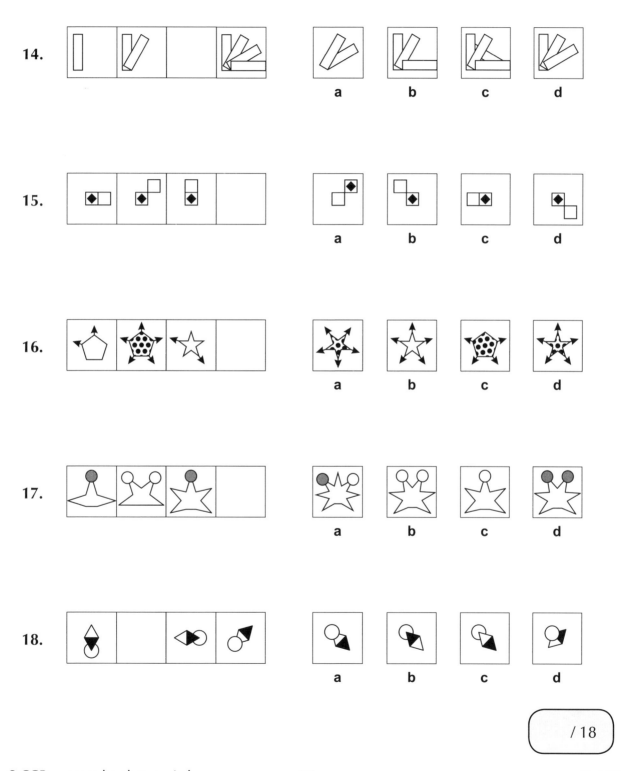

14.

a   b   c   d

15.

a   b   c   d

16.

a   b   c   d

17.

a   b   c   d

18.

a   b   c   d

/ 18

Have a go at these puzzles — they're a great way to practise **spotting similarities**.

Superhero Line-Up

Max draws two superhero characters. Each superhero eats special power food and each one has a sidekick. He wants to draw a new superhero, food and sidekick that is most like the other two superheroes, food and sidekick.

Circle the superhero, food and sidekick he draws.

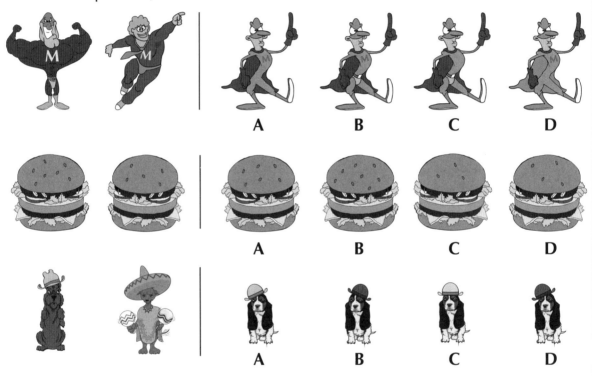

Flying the Flag

Emily has a set of four flags that form a series. Draw her second flag.

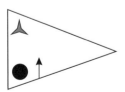 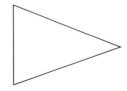 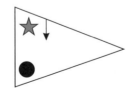 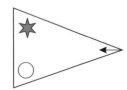

Test 16

You have **10 minutes** to do this test. Circle the letter for each correct answer.

Work out which option would look like the figure on the left if it was reflected over the line.

Reflect

1.

          a   b   c   d

Reflect

2.

          a   b   c   d

Reflect

3.

          a   b   c   d

Reflect

4.

          a   b   c   d

Reflect

5.

          a   b   c   d

Look at how the first bug changes to become the second bug. Then work out which option would look like the third bug if you changed it in the same way.

6.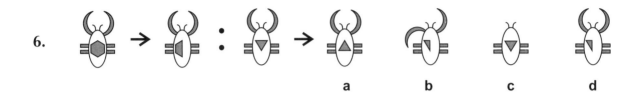

                                                  a   b   c   d

7, 8.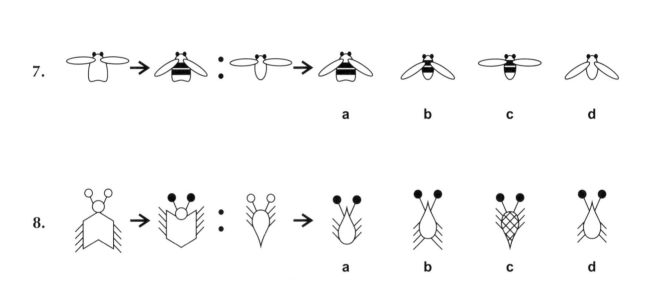

9.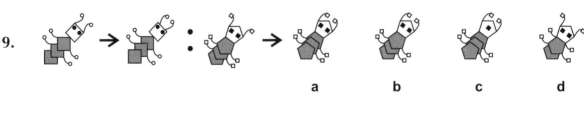

10.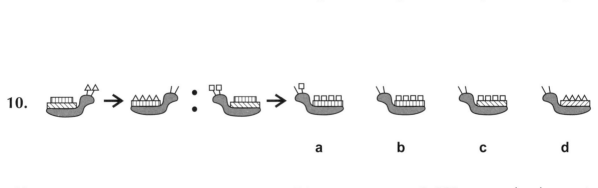

Work out which of the four cubes can be made from the net.

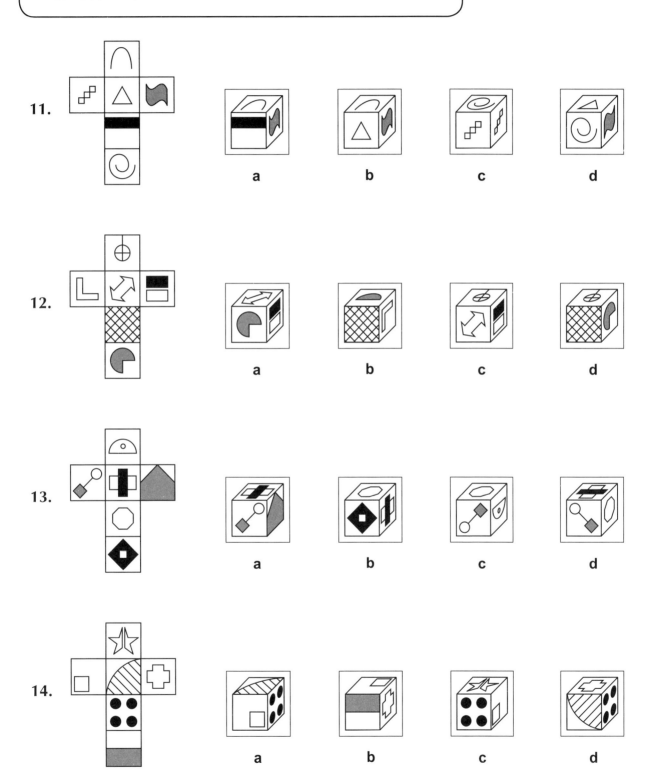

11.

a   b   c   d

12.

a   b   c   d

13.

a   b   c   d

14.

a   b   c   d

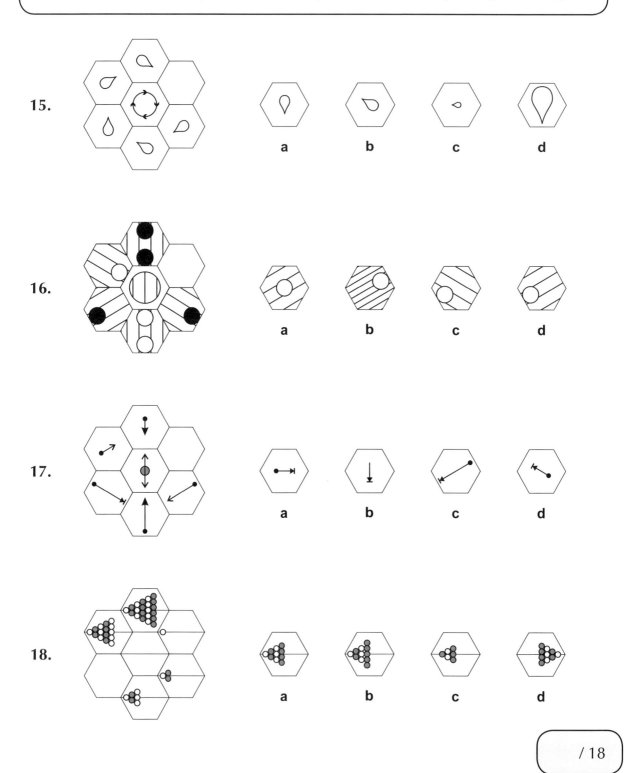

15. a b c d

16. a b c d

17. a b c d

18. a b c d

/ 18

Test 17

You have **10 minutes** to do this test. Circle the letter for each correct answer.

Work out which 3D figure in the grey box has been rotated to make the new 3D figure.

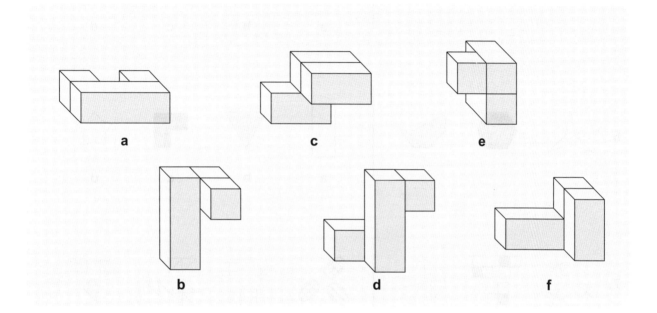

a   c   e

b   d   f

1.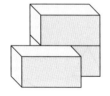

a   d

b   e

c   f

2.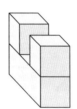

a   d

b   e

c   f

3.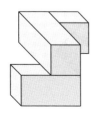

a   d

b   e

c   f

4.

a   d

b   e

c   f

77

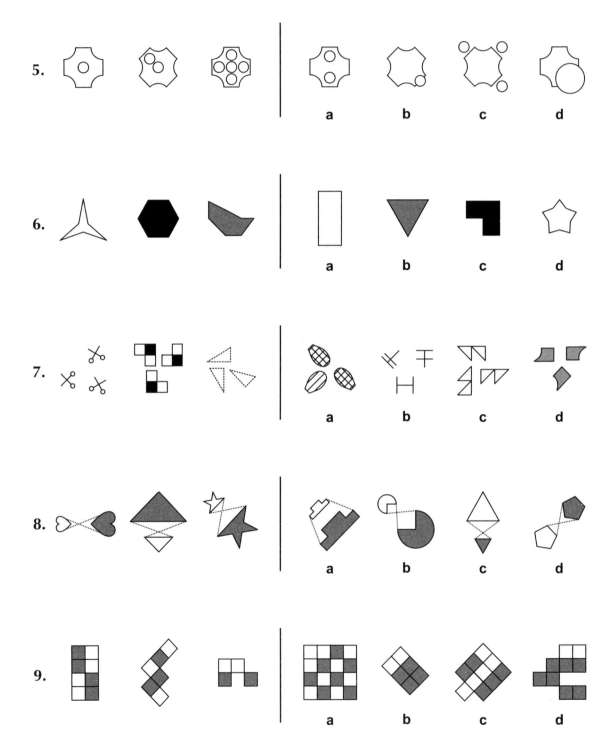

5.

    a   b   c   d

6.

    a   b   c   d

7.

    a   b   c   d

8.

    a   b   c   d

9.

    a   b   c   d

Work out which of the options best fits in place of the missing hexagon in the grid.

10.

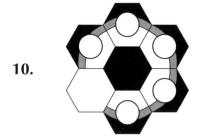

a

b

c

d

11.

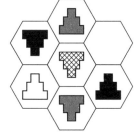

a

b

c

d

12.

a

b

c

d

13.

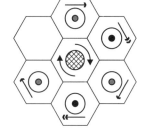

a

b

c

d

Test 17

Look at how the first two figures are changed, and then work out which option would look like the third figure if you changed it in the same way.

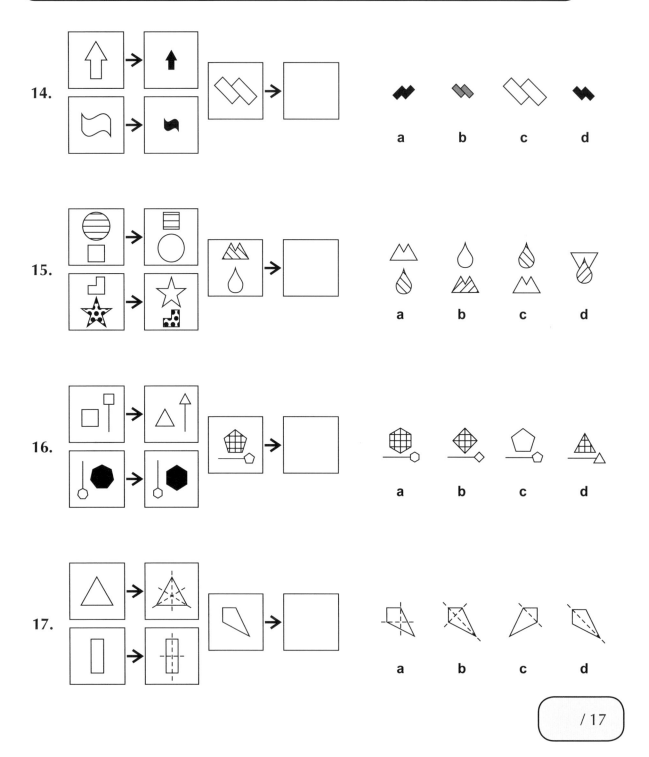

14.

a   b   c   d

15.

a   b   c   d

16.

a   b   c   d

17.

a   b   c   d

/ 17

Test 18

You have **10 minutes** to do this test. Circle the letter for each correct answer.

Work out which of the options best fits in place of the missing square in the series.

1.

                                             a   **b**   **c**   **d**

2.

                                             a   **b**   **c**   **d**

3.

                                             a   **b**   **c**   **d**

4.
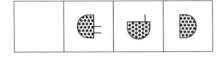

                                             a   **b**   **c**   **d**

5.

                                             a   **b**   **c**   **d**

Work out which option would look like the figure on the left if it was rotated.

Rotate

6.

                                 a   b   c   d

Rotate

7.

                                 a   b   c   d

Rotate

8.

                                 a   b   c   d

Rotate

9.

                                 a   b   c   d

Rotate

10.

                                 a   b   c   d

Work out which of the four cubes can be made from the net.

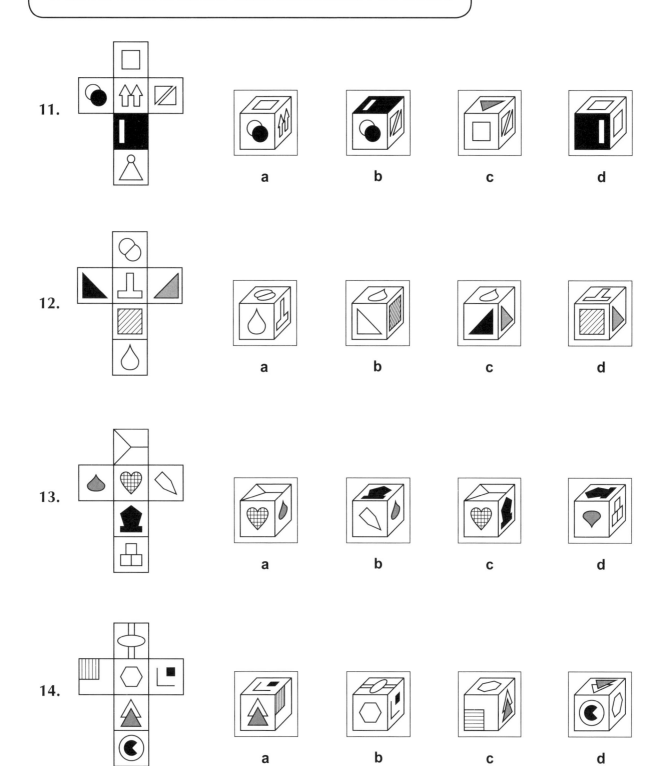

11.   a   b   c   d

12.   a   b   c   d

13.   a   b   c   d

14.   a   b   c   d

83

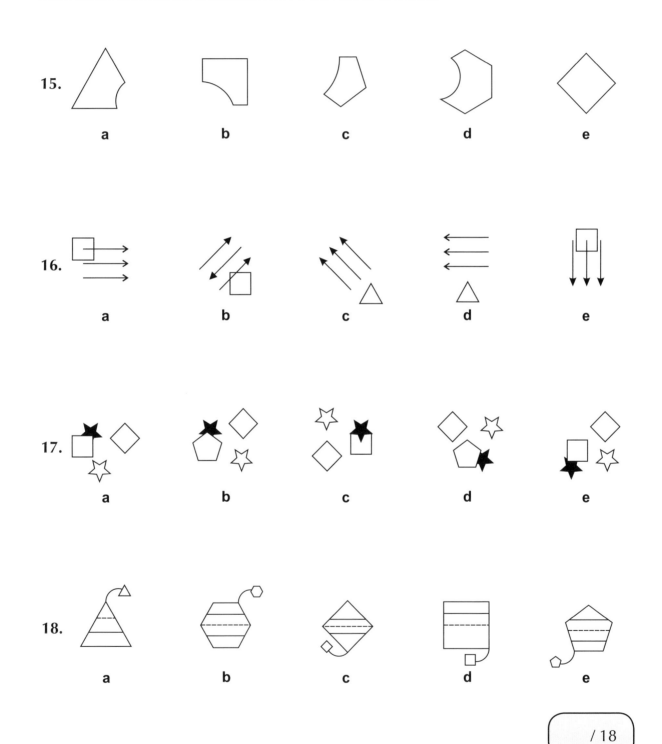

15. a b c d e

16. a b c d e

17. a b c d e

18. a b c d e

/ 18

Puzzles 6

These puzzles are all about **3D shapes** — jump right in and test your skills!

Winging It...

Rimi builds a robot butterfly out of blocks. It should have four wings, but it is missing one. Which figure will make her butterfly below symmetrical again?

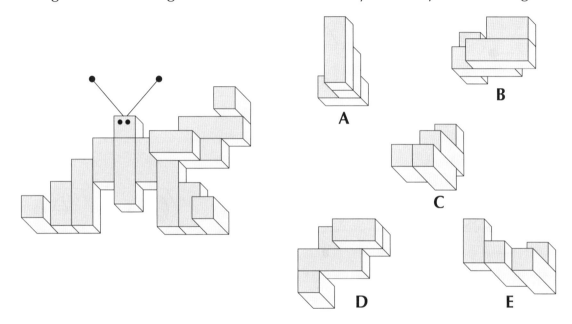

The Leaning Tower of Pizza

Martin has made a tower out of pizza boxes, salad boxes and garlic bread boxes as shown on the right.

How many of each box has he used?

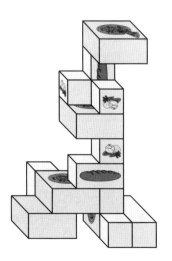

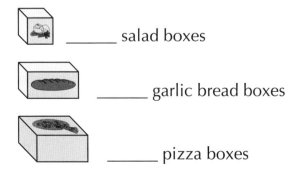

_____ salad boxes

_____ garlic bread boxes

_____ pizza boxes

Puzzles 6

You have **10 minutes** to do this test. Circle the letter for each correct answer.

Work out which of the options best fits in place of the missing hexagon in the grid.

1.

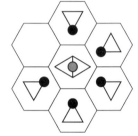

a   b   c   d

2.

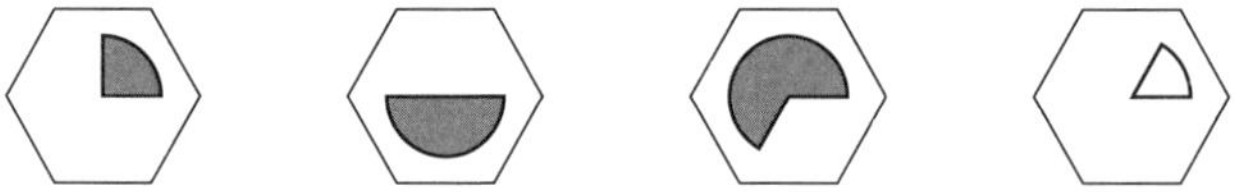

a   b   c   d

3.

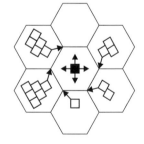

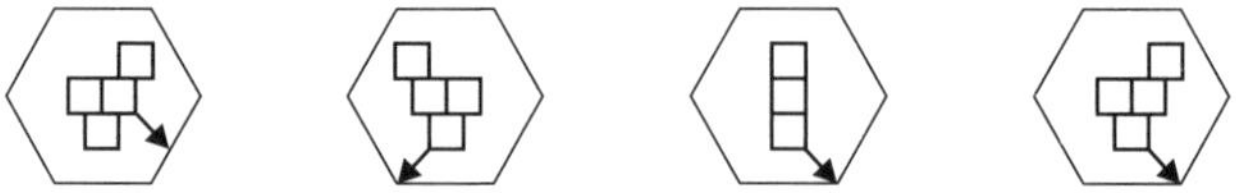

a   b   c   d

4.

a   b   c   d

Work out which 3D figure in the grey box has been rotated to make the new 3D figure.

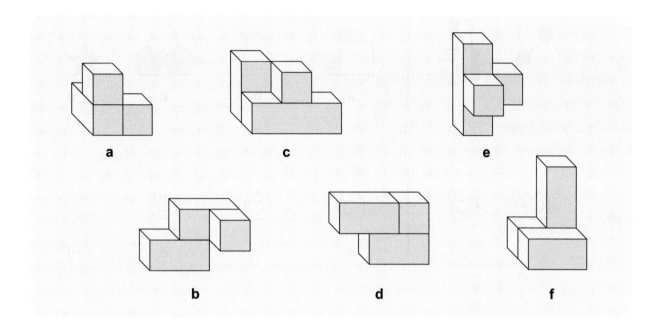

a

c

e

b

d

f

5.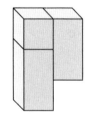

a   d

b   e

c   f

6.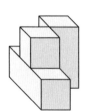

a   d

b   e

c   f

7.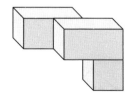

a   d

b   e

c   f

8.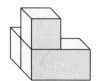

a   d

b   e

c   f

Work out which option is most like the two figures on the left.

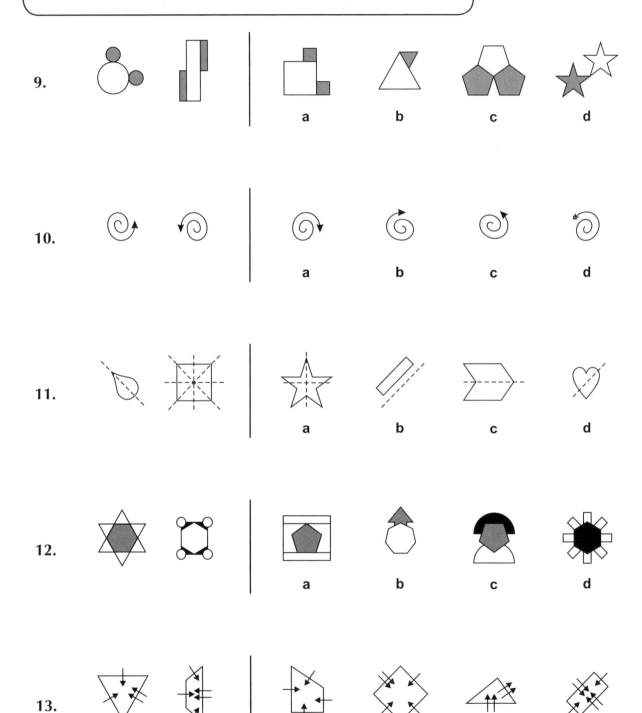

9.

a b c d

10.

a b c d

11.

a b c d

12.

a b c d

13.

a b c d

Look at how the first two figures are changed, and then work out which option would look like the third figure if you changed it in the same way.

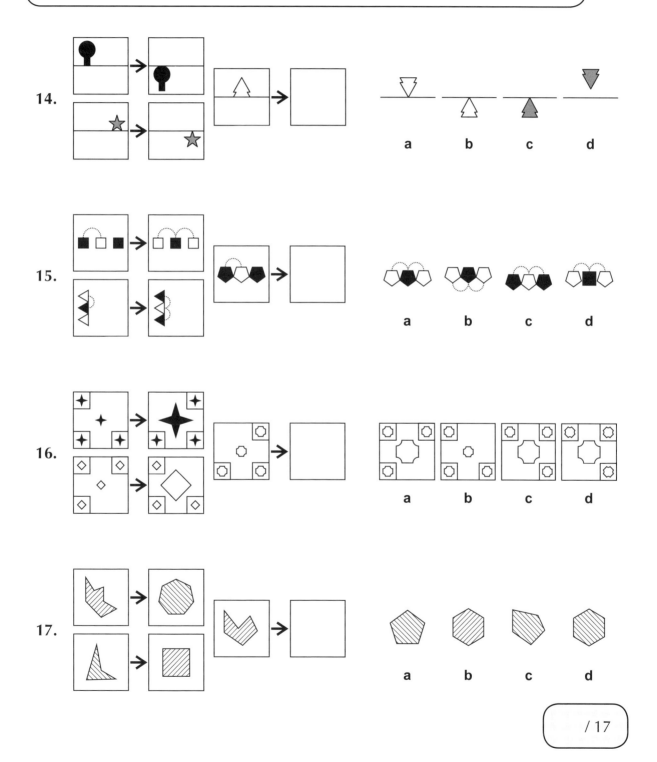

14.

a   b   c   d

15.

a   b   c   d

16.

a   b   c   d

17.

a   b   c   d

/ 17

89

You have **10 minutes** to do this test. Circle the letter for each correct answer.

Work out which 3D figure in the grey box has been rotated to make the new 3D figure.

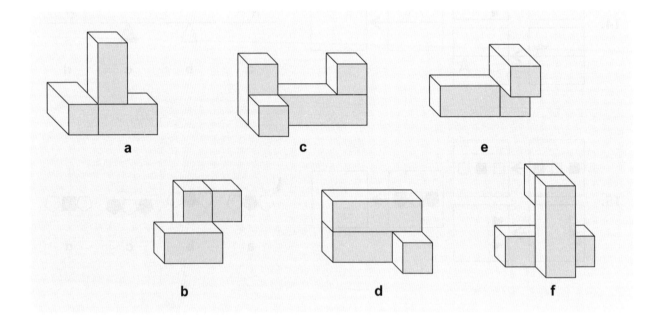

a

c

e

b

d

f

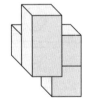

1.

a	d
b	e
c	f

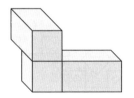

2.

a	d
b	e
c	f

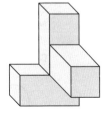

3.

a	d
b	e
c	f

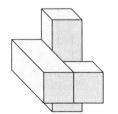

4.

a	d
b	e
c	f

Work out which option is most like the two figures on the left.

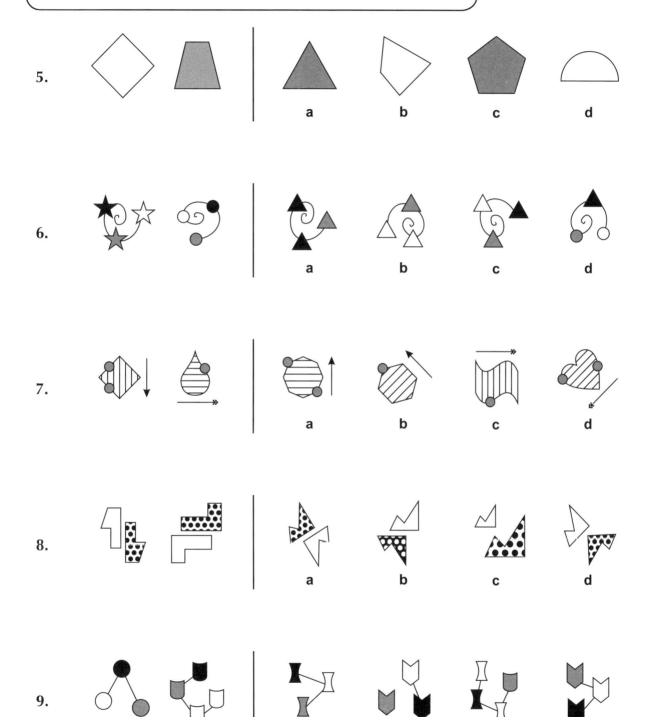

5.

               a   b   c   d

6.

               a   b   c   d

7.

               a   b   c   d

8.

               a   b   c   d

9.

               a   b   c   d

Work out which option would look like the figure on the left if it was reflected over the line.

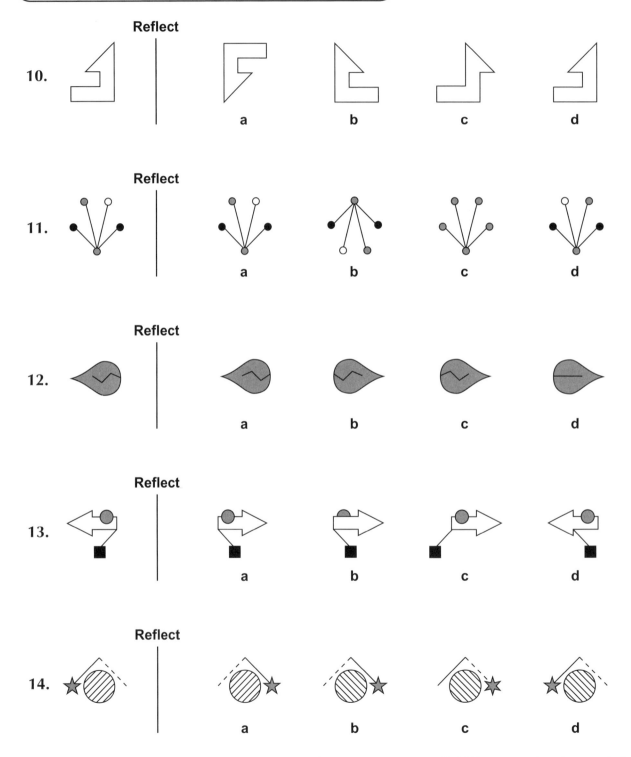

Reflect

10.

    a   b   c   d

Reflect

11.

    a   b   c   d

Reflect

12.

    a   b   c   d

Reflect

13.

    a   b   c   d

Reflect

14.

    a   b   c   d

Work out which of the options best fits in place of the missing square in the grid.

15.

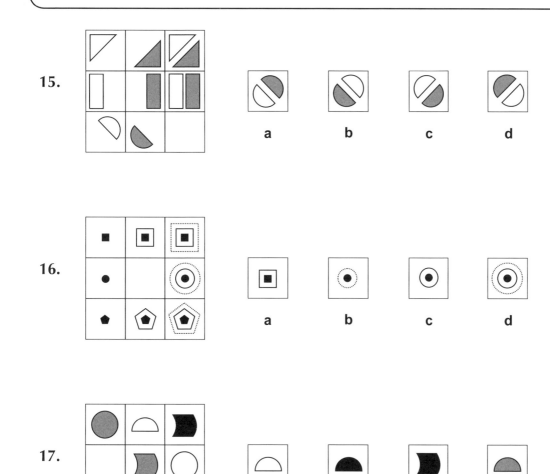

16.

17.

18.

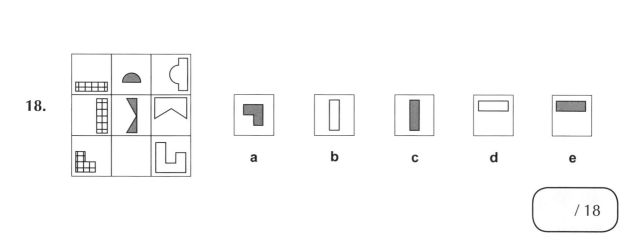

/ 18

You have **10 minutes** to do this test. Circle the letter for each correct answer.

Find the figure in each row that is most unlike the others.

1.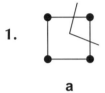

    a   **b**   **c**   **d**   **e**

2.

    a   **b**   **c**   **d**   **e**

3.

    a   **b**   **c**   **d**   **e**

4.

    a   **b**   **c**   **d**   **e**

Work out which option would look like the figure on the left if it was rotated.

5.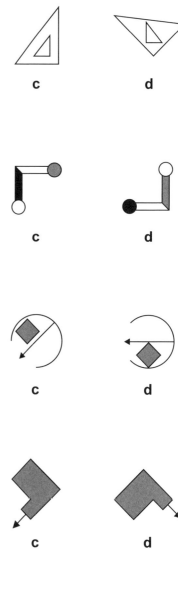

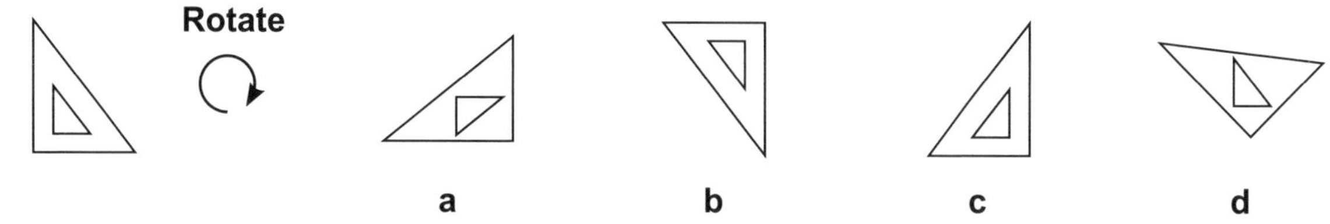

Rotate

a   b   c   d

6. **Rotate**

a   b   c   d

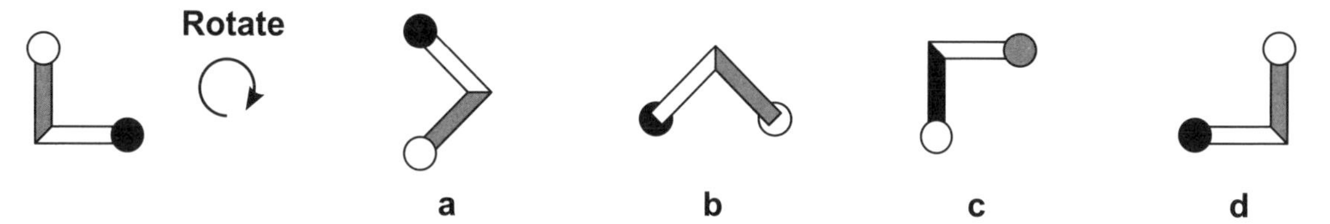

7. **Rotate**

a   b   c   d

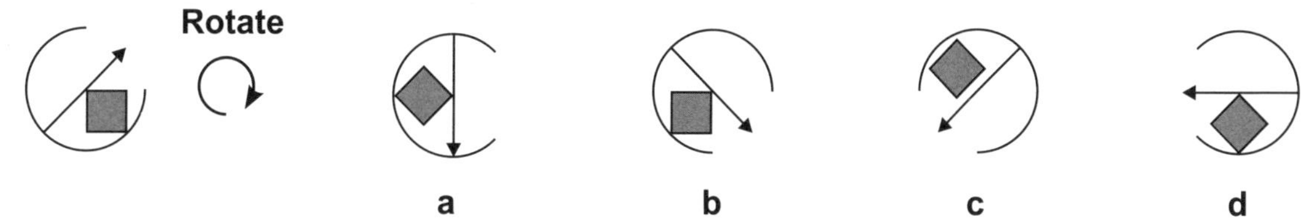

8. **Rotate**

a   b   c   d

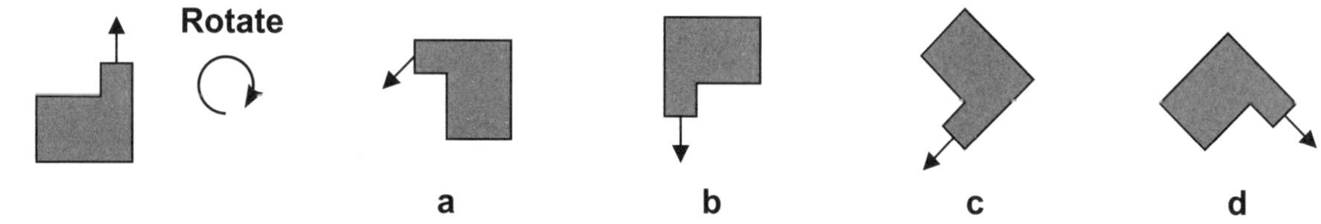

9. **Rotate**

a   b   c   d

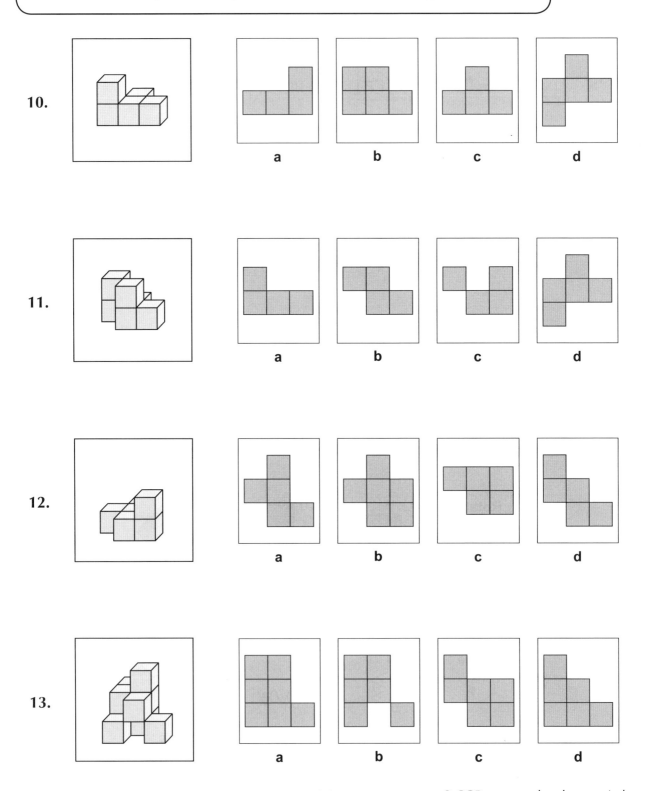

10.

a   b   c   d

11.

a   b   c   d

12.

a   b   c   d

13.

a   b   c   d

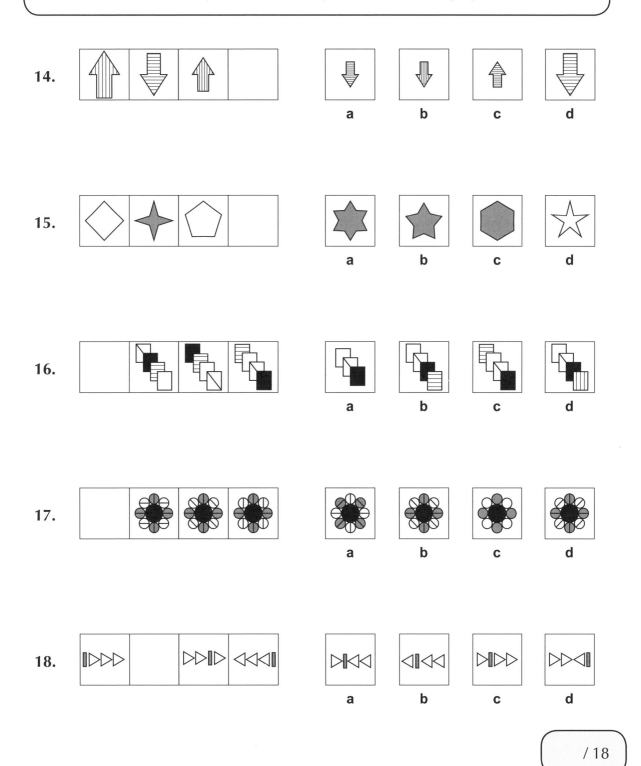

14.

        a   b   c   d

15.

        a   b   c   d

16.

        a   b   c   d

17.

        a   b   c   d

18.

        a   b   c   d

/ 18

Test 21

Time for a break! This puzzle is ideal for practising your **sequencing** skills.

Let's Play Rain Chain!

<u>Rain Chain</u> is a card game. Each card in the game shows blue raindrops along the top and a black or striped shape in the middle.

To play a card, you have to follow the Rain Chain rules.

Your card must have <u>all</u> of the following:

- <u>One more</u> or <u>one less</u> raindrop than the last card played.
- A shape with <u>one more</u> or <u>one less</u> side than the shape on the last card played.
- A black shape if the last card played was striped.
- A striped shape if the last card played was black.

Here is a hand of five cards. Draw lines to show which card or cards you could play on each of the four cards at the bottom.

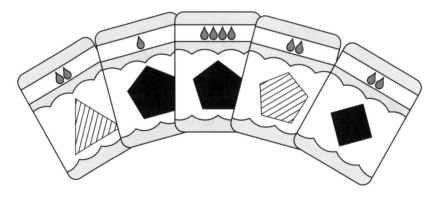

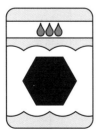   

98

You have **10 minutes** to do this test. Circle the letter for each correct answer.

Work out which option would look like the figure on the left if it was rotated.

Rotate

1.

a

b

c

d

Rotate

2.

a

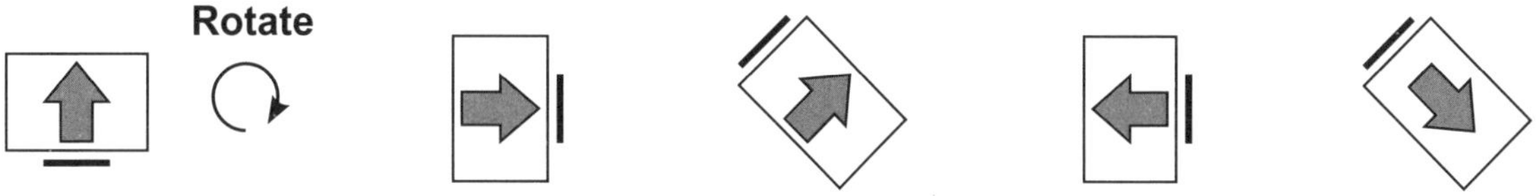

b

c

d

Rotate

3.

a

b

c

d

Rotate

4.

a

b

c

d

Rotate

5.

a

b

c

d

Work out which of the four cubes can be made from the net.

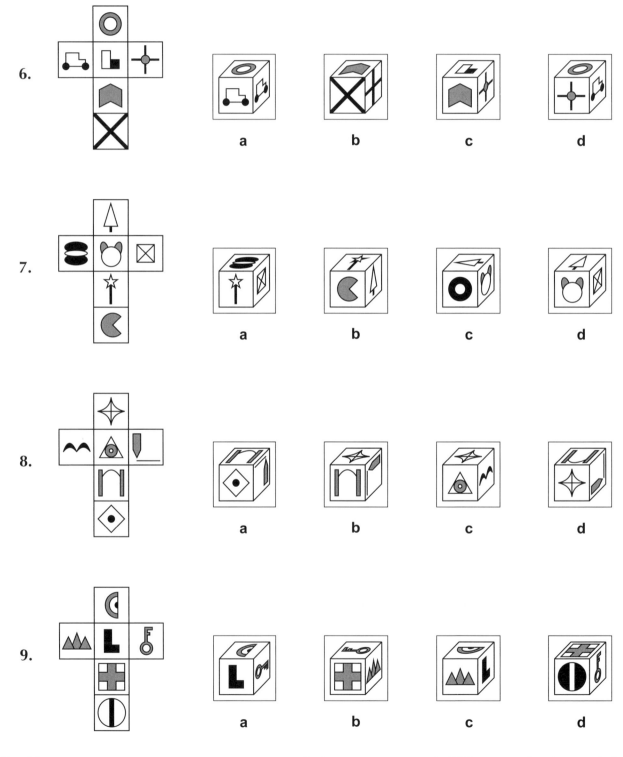

6.   a   b   c   d

7.   a   b   c   d

8.   a   b   c   d

9.   a   b   c   d

Work out which option is most like the three figures on the left.

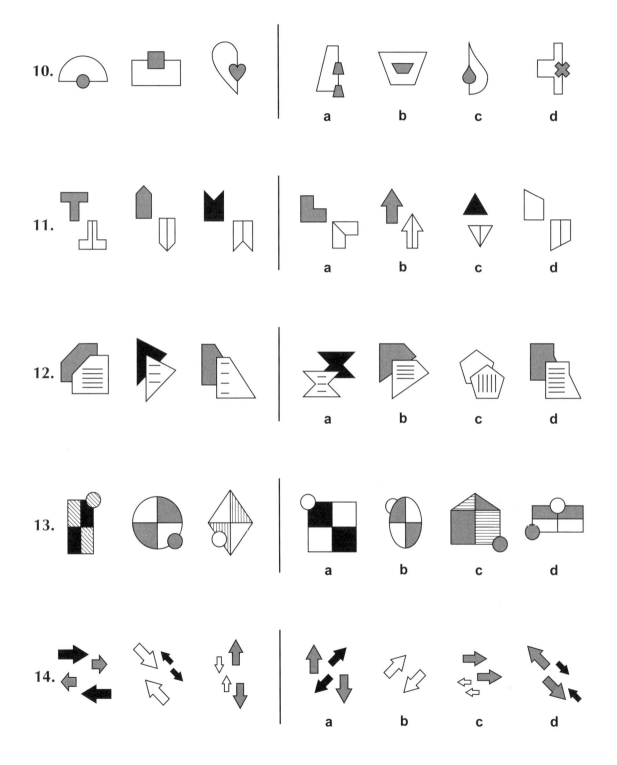

10.	a	b	c	d

11.	a	b	c	d

12.	a	b	c	d

13.	a	b	c	d

14.	a	b	c	d

Work out which of the options best fits in place of the missing square in the grid.

15.

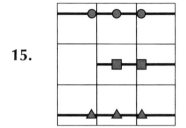

a   b   c   d   e

16.

a   b   c   d   e

17.

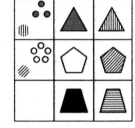

a   b   c   d   e

18.

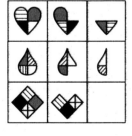

a   b   c   d   e

/ 18

Test 23

You have **10 minutes** to do this test. Circle the letter for each correct answer.

Find the figure in each row that is most unlike the others.

1.

a

b

c

d

e

2.

a

b

c

d

e

3.

a

b

c

d

e

4.

a

b

c

d

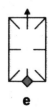
e

103

Work out which of the options best fits in place of the missing square in the grid.

5.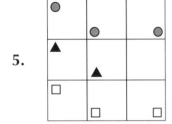

a   b   c   d   e

6.

a   b   c   d   e

7.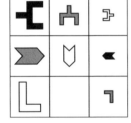

a   b   c   d   e

8.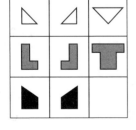

a   b   c   d   e

Work out which option would look like the figure on the left if it was reflected over the line.

Reflect

9.

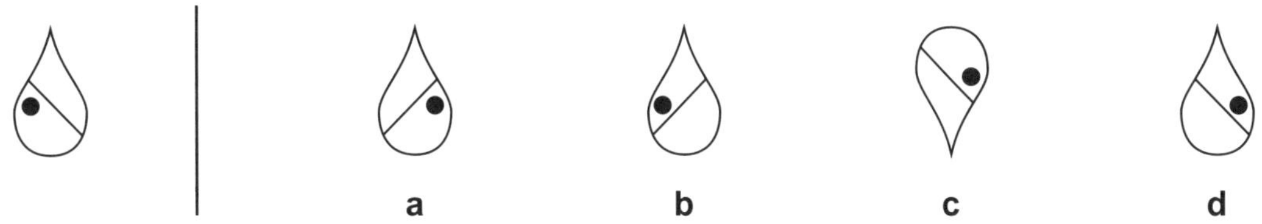

a   b   c   d

Reflect

10.

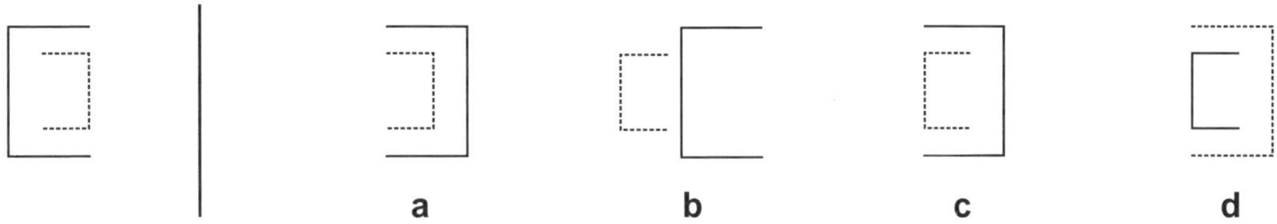

a   b   c   d

Reflect

11.

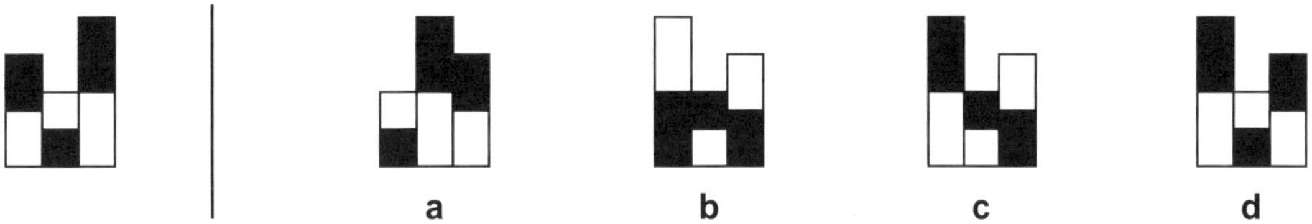

a   b   c   d

Reflect

12.

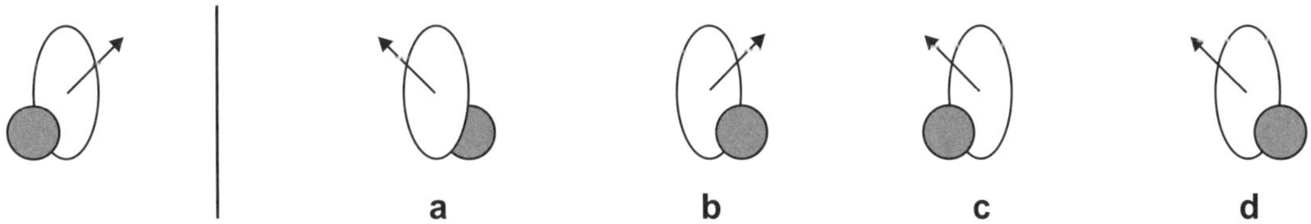

a   b   c   d

Reflect

13.

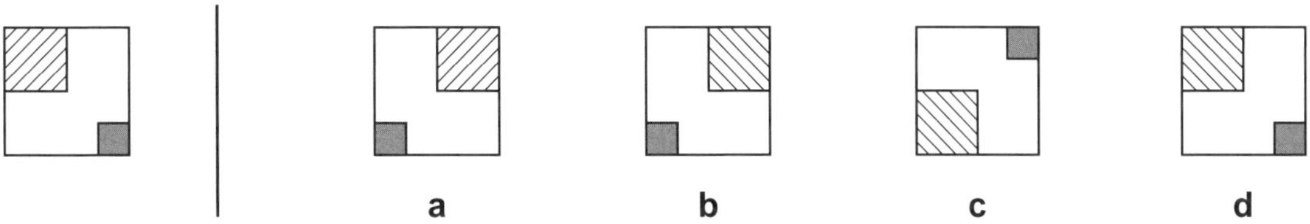

a   b   c   d

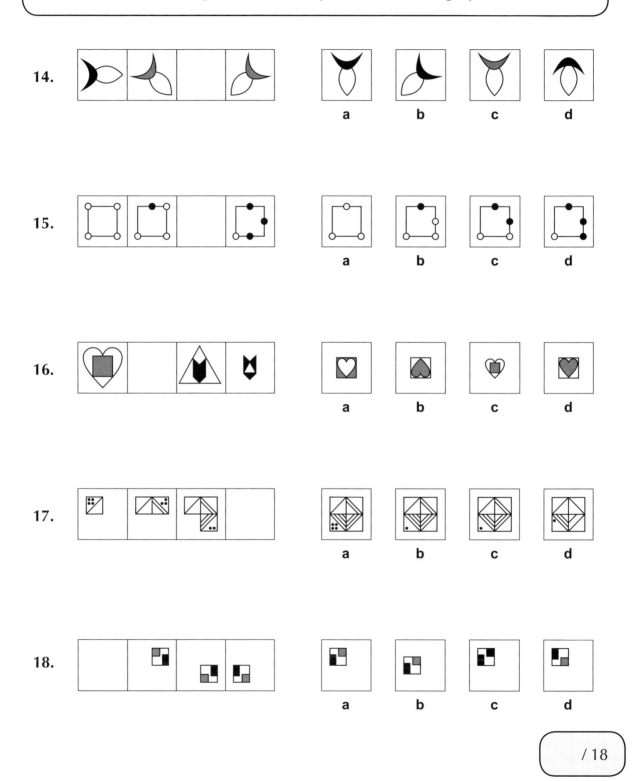

14.

a   b   c   d

15.

a   b   c   d

16.

a   b   c   d

17.

a   b   c   d

18.

a   b   c   d

/ 18

Test 24

You have **10 minutes** to do this test. Circle the letter for each correct answer.

Look at how the first two figures are changed, and then work out which option would look like the third figure if you changed it in the same way.

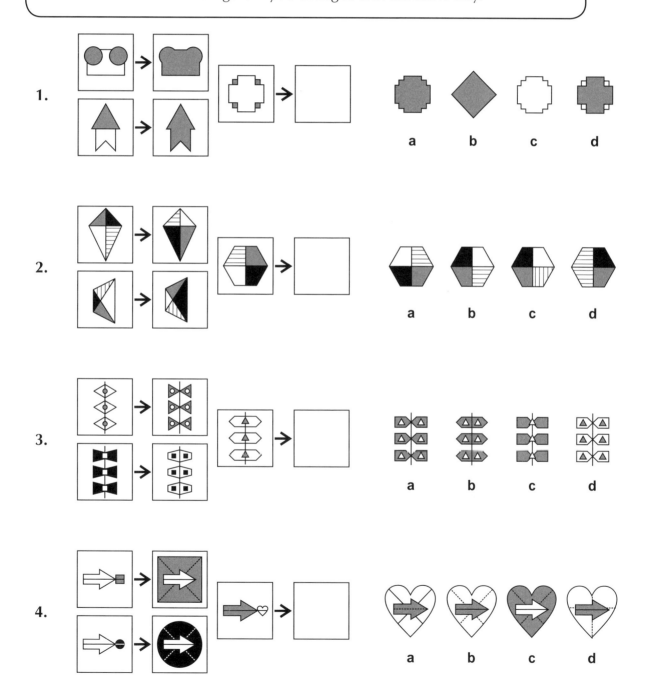

© CGP — not to be photocopied   107   Test 24

Work out which of the options best fits in place of the missing square in the series.

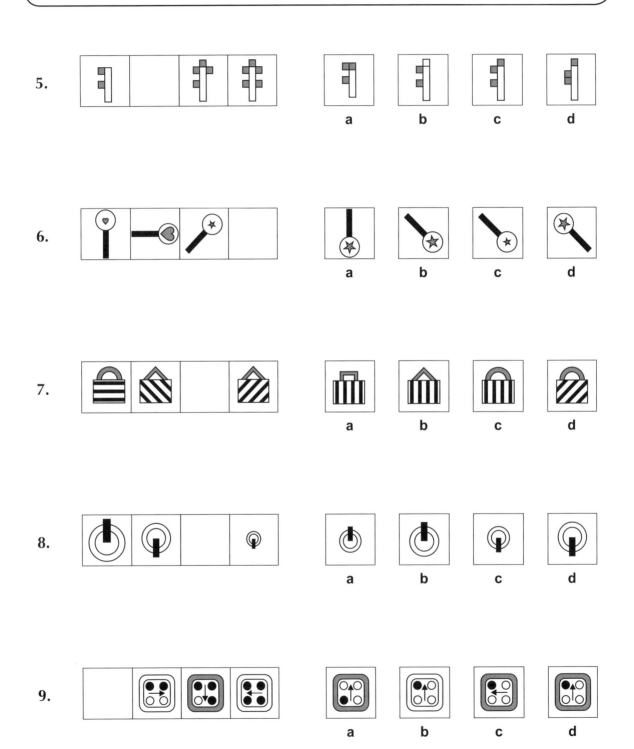

5.

a   b   c   d

6.

a   b   c   d

7.

a   b   c   d

8.

a   b   c   d

9.

a   b   c   d

Work out which of the four cubes can be made from the net.

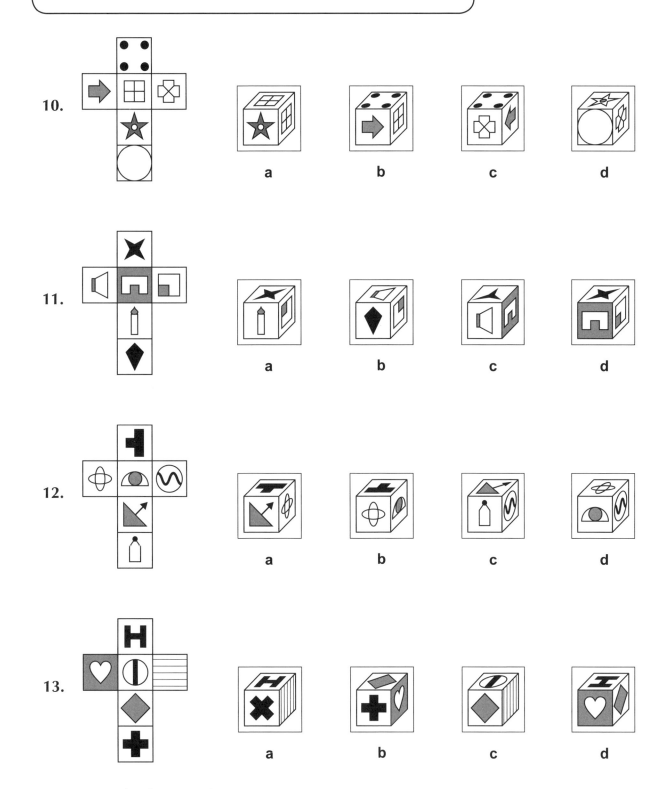

10.

a   b   c   d

11.

a   b   c   d

12.

a   b   c   d

13.

a   b   c   d

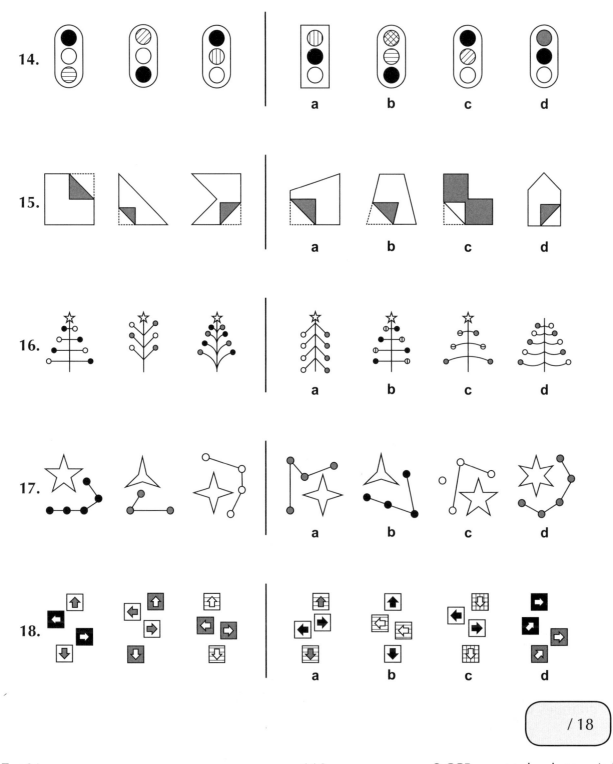

14.

a b c d

15.

a b c d

16.

a b c d

17.

a b c d

18.

a b c d

/ 18

Puzzles 8

These puzzles are brilliant for practising some of the skills you'll need.

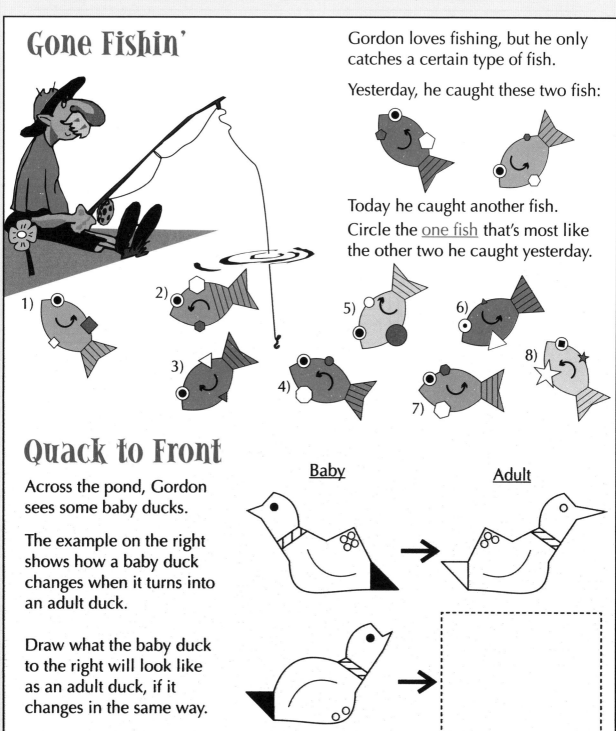

Gone Fishin'

Gordon loves fishing, but he only catches a certain type of fish.

Yesterday, he caught these two fish:

Today he caught another fish.
Circle the <u>one fish</u> that's most like the other two he caught yesterday.

1)

2)

3)

4)

5)

6)

7)

8)

Quack to Front

Across the pond, Gordon sees some baby ducks.

The example on the right shows how a baby duck changes when it turns into an adult duck.

Draw what the baby duck to the right will look like as an adult duck, if it changes in the same way.

<u>Baby</u>

<u>Adult</u>

111

Test 25

You have **10 minutes** to do this test. Circle the letter for each correct answer.

Work out which set of blocks can be put together to make the 3D figure on the left.

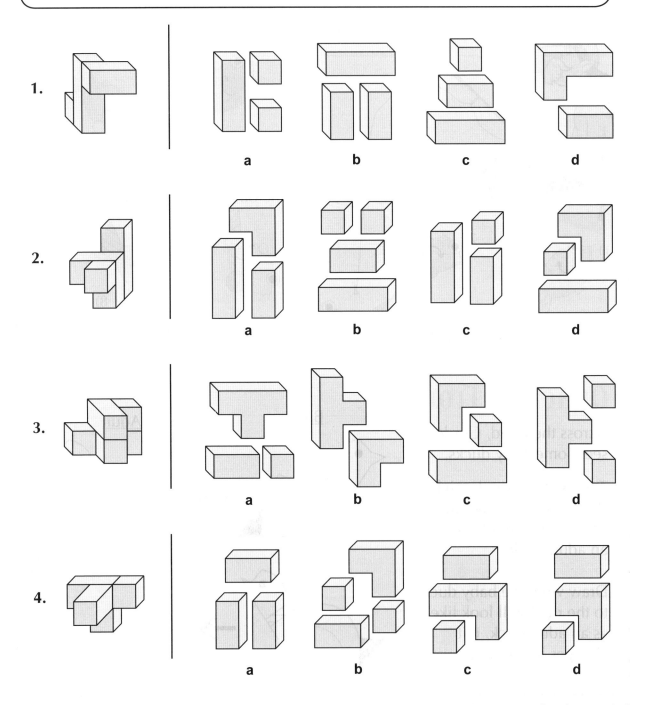

Work out which of the options best fits in place of the missing hexagon in the grid.

5.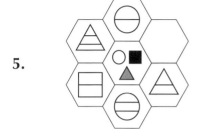

a   b   c   d

6.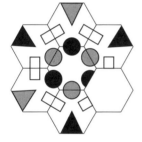

a   b   c   d

7.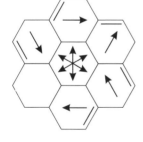

a   b   c   d

8.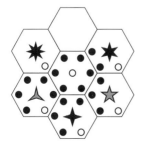

a   b   c   d

Work out which of the options best fits in place of the missing square in the series.

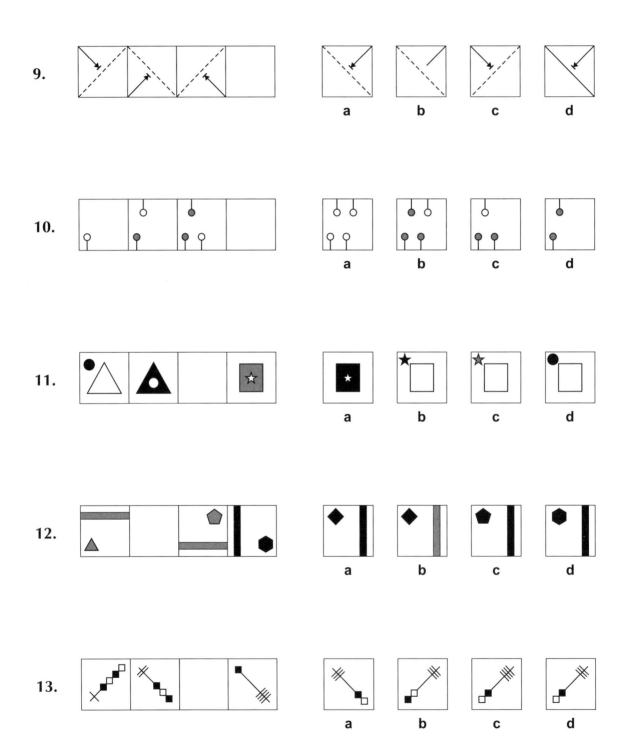

9.

a b c d

10.

a b c d

11.

a b c d

12.

a b c d

13.

a b c d

114

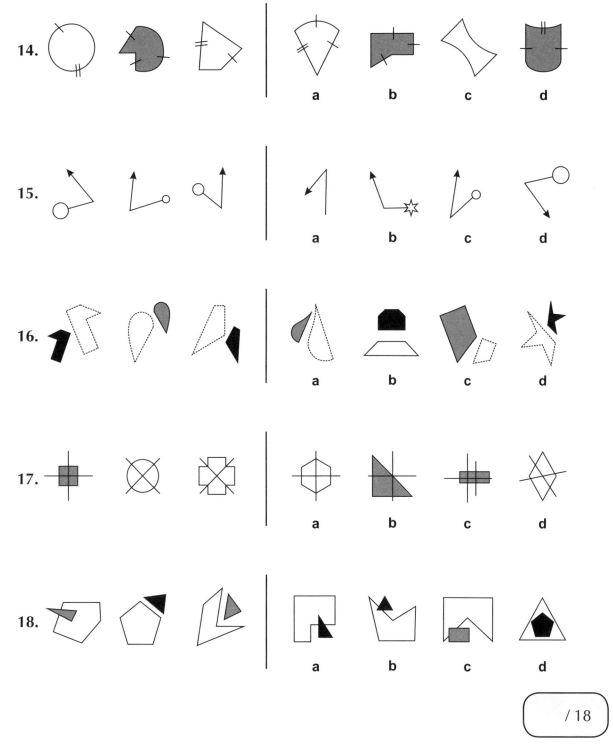

14. a b c d

15. a b c d

16. a b c d

17. a b c d

18. a b c d

/ 18

You have **10 minutes** to do this test. Circle the letter for each correct answer.

Work out which option would look like the figure
on the left if it was reflected over the line.

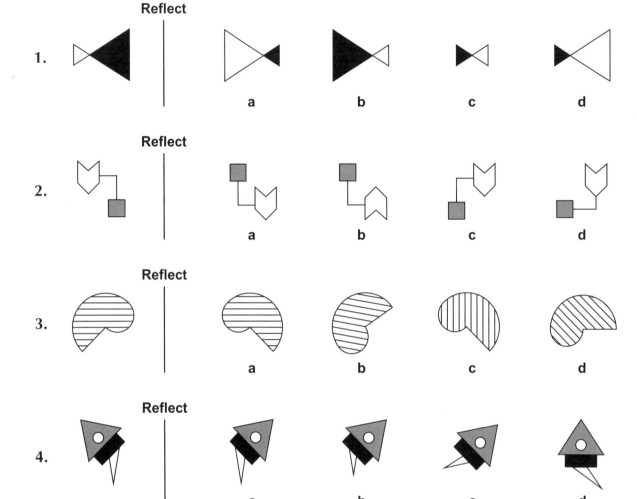

Reflect

1.

         a   b   c   d

Reflect

2.

         a   b   c   d

Reflect

3.

         a   b   c   d

Reflect

4.

         a   b   c   d

Reflect

5.

         a   b   c   d

Work out which of the options best fits in place of the missing square in the grid.

6.

    a   b   c   d   e

7.

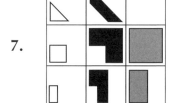

    a   b   c   d   e

8.

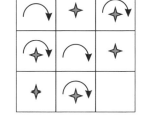

    a   b   c   d   e

9.

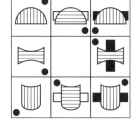

    a   b   c   d   e

Test 26

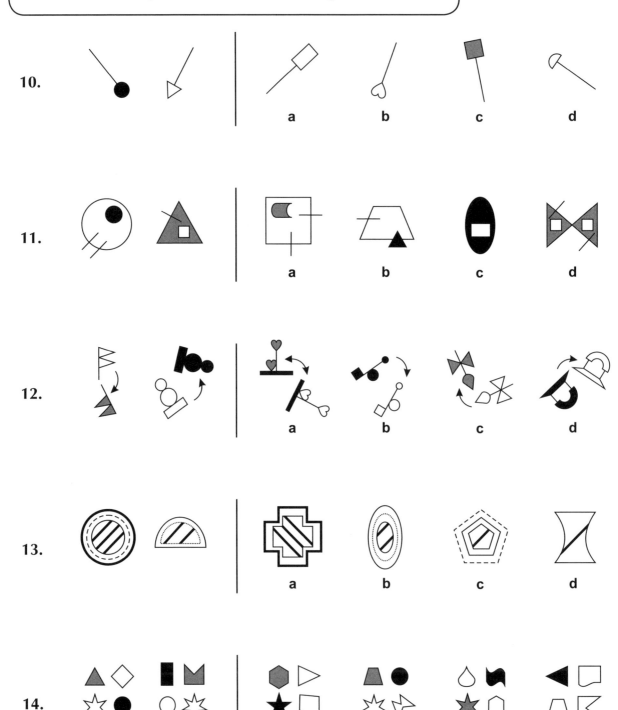

10.

a   b   c   d

11.

a   b   c   d

12.

a   b   c   d

13.

a   b   c   d

14.

a   b   c   d

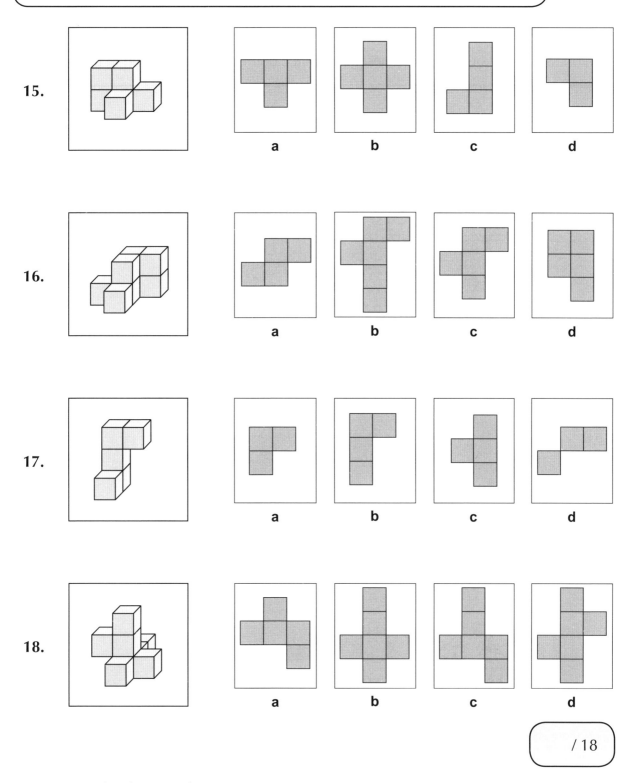

15.

a   b   c   d

16.

a   b   c   d

17.

a   b   c   d

18.

a   b   c   d

/ 18

Test 27

You have **10 minutes** to do this test. Circle the letter for each correct answer.

Work out which of the options best fits in place of the missing hexagon in the grid.

1.

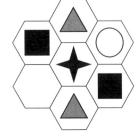

a　　　　b　　　　c　　　　d

2.

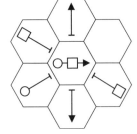

a　　　　b　　　　c　　　　d

3.

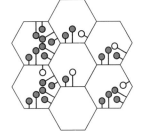

a　　　　b　　　　c　　　　d

4.

a　　　　b　　　　c　　　　d

Find the figure in each row that is most unlike the others.

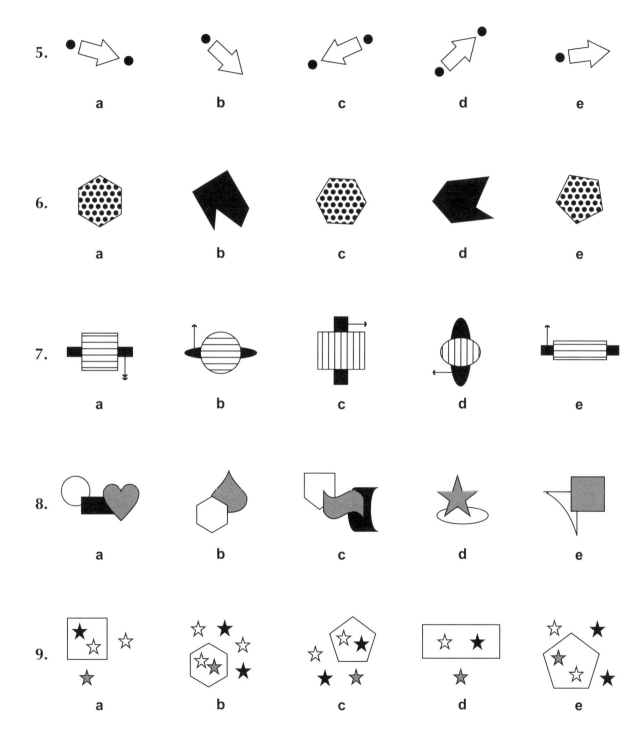

5.   a   b   c   d   e

6.   a   b   c   d   e

7.   a   b   c   d   e

8.   a   b   c   d   e

9.   a   b   c   d   e

121

Work out which 3D figure in the grey box has been rotated to make the new 3D figure.

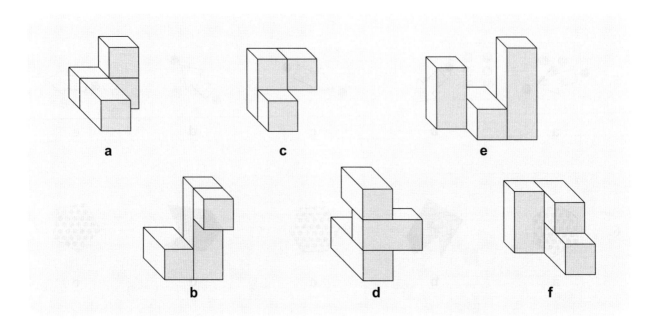

a

c

e

b

d

f

10.

a   d

b   e

c   f

11.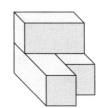

a   d

b   e

c   f

12.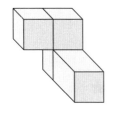

a   d

b   e

c   f

13.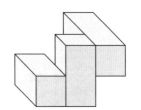

a   d

b   e

c   f

Look at how the first two figures are changed, and then work out which option would look like the third figure if you changed it in the same way.

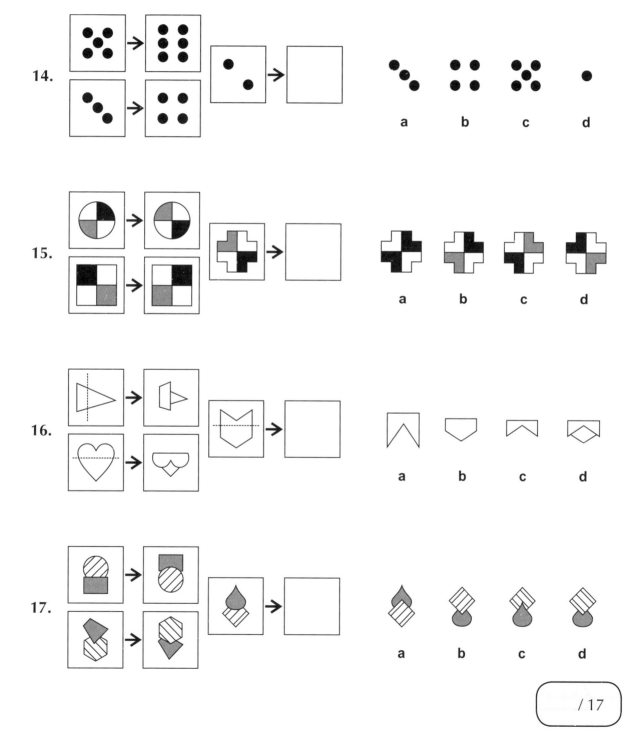

14.

a   b   c   d

15.

a   b   c   d

16.

a   b   c   d

17.

a   b   c   d

/ 17

123

Puzzles 9

Rotating shapes and nets are what these puzzles are all about — give them a go!

I-tentacle Twins

A group of aliens have fallen from their spaceship. Circle the <u>two</u> identical aliens.

Christmas Pyramids

Lukas is making decorations in the shape of a pyramid to hang from the Christmas tree.
He uses the net shown below.

Circle the decoration he makes.

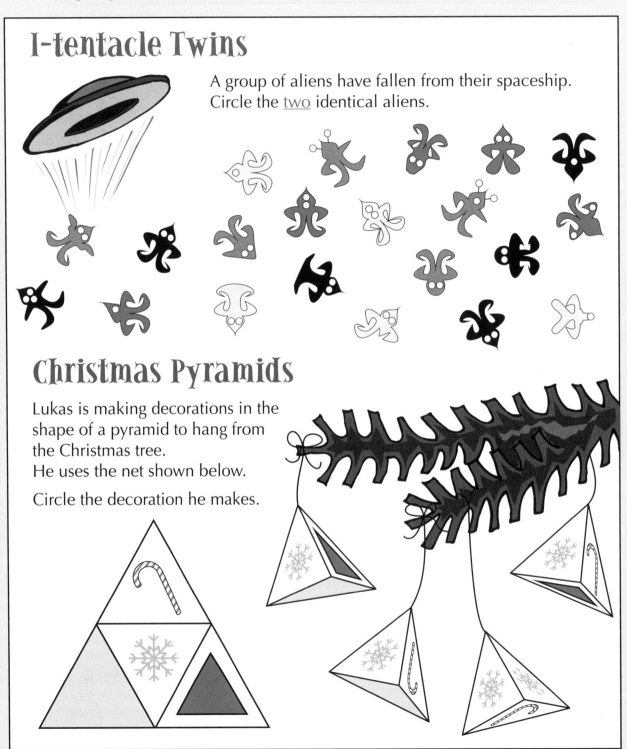

You have **10 minutes** to do this test. Circle the letter for each correct answer.

Work out which of the options best fits in place of the missing square in the grid.

1.

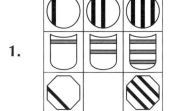

  a

  b

  c

  d

  e

2.

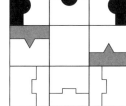

  a

b

  c

d

  e

3.

  a

  b

  c

  d

  e

4.

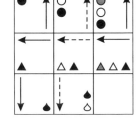

  a

  b

  c

  d

  e

125

Work out which option is most like the two figures on the left.

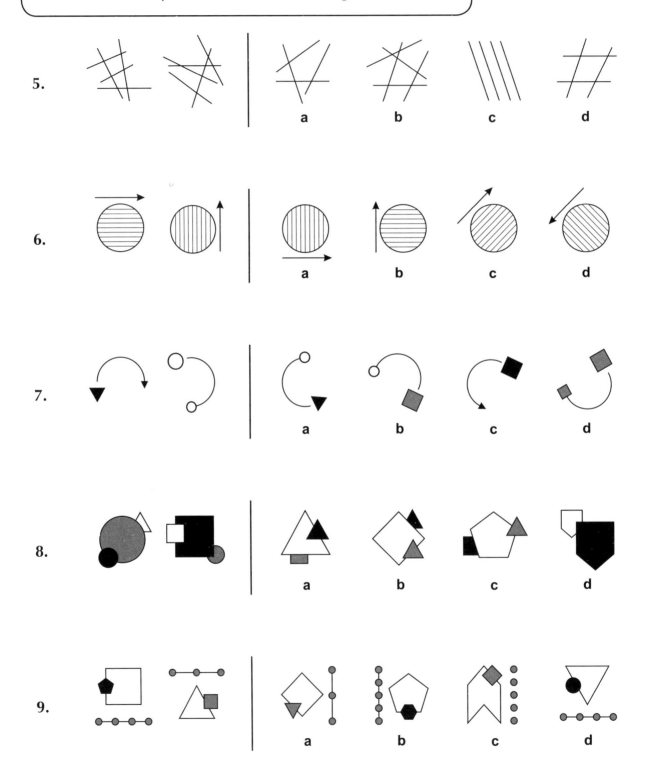

5.

a   b   c   d

6.

a   b   c   d

7.

a   b   c   d

8.

a   b   c   d

9.

a   b   c   d

Work out which 3D figure in the grey box has been rotated to make the new 3D figure.

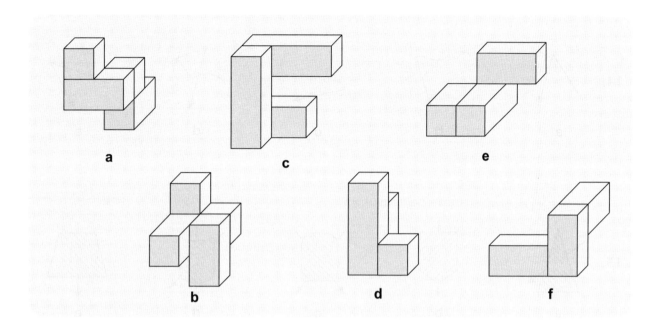

a   b   c   d   e   f

10.

a	d
b	e
c	f

11.

a	d
b	e
c	f

12.

a	d
b	e
c	f

13.

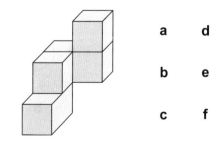

a	d
b	e
c	f

Test 28

Find the figure in each row that is most unlike the others.

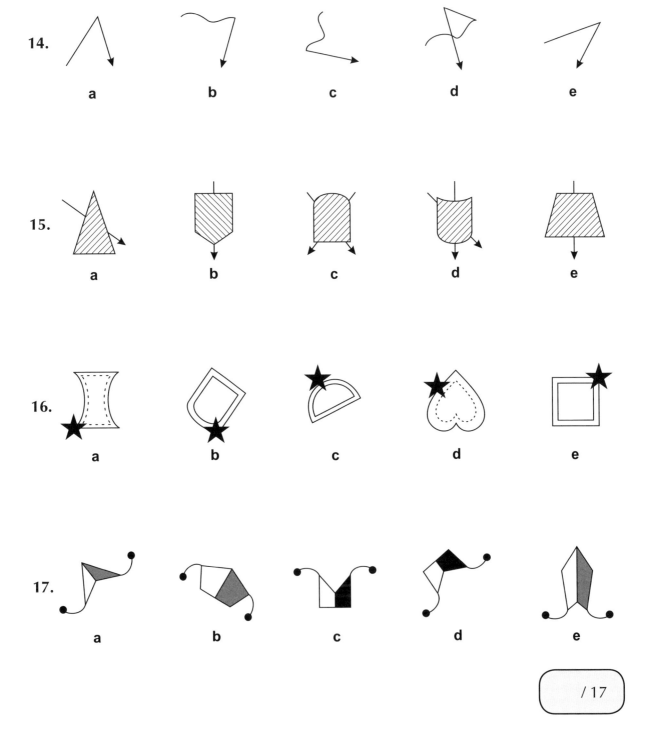

14.

    a   b   c   d   e

15.

    a   b   c   d   e

16.

    a   b   c   d   e

17.

    a   b   c   d   e

/ 17

Test 29

You have **10 minutes** to do this test. Circle the letter for each correct answer.

Work out which option is most like the three figures on the left.

1. |

                                                       a   **b**   **c**   **d**

2. |

                                                         a   **b**   **c**   **d**

3. |

                                                         a   **b**   **c**   **d**

4. |

                                                         a   **b**   **c**   **d**

5. |

                                                         a   **b**   **c**   **d**

Work out which option is a top-down 2D view of the 3D figure on the left.

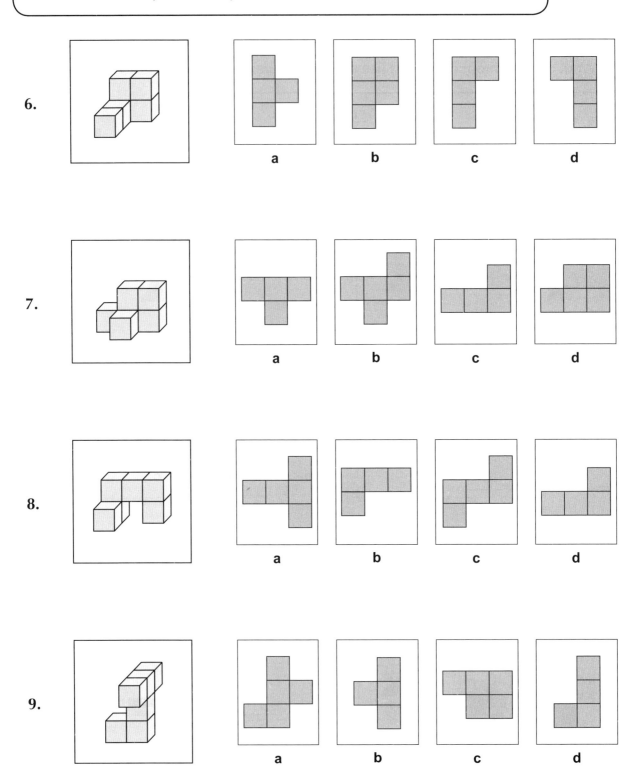

6.

a   b   c   d

7.

a   b   c   d

8.

a   b   c   d

9.

a   b   c   d

130

Look at how the first two figures are changed, and then work out which option would look like the third figure if you changed it in the same way.

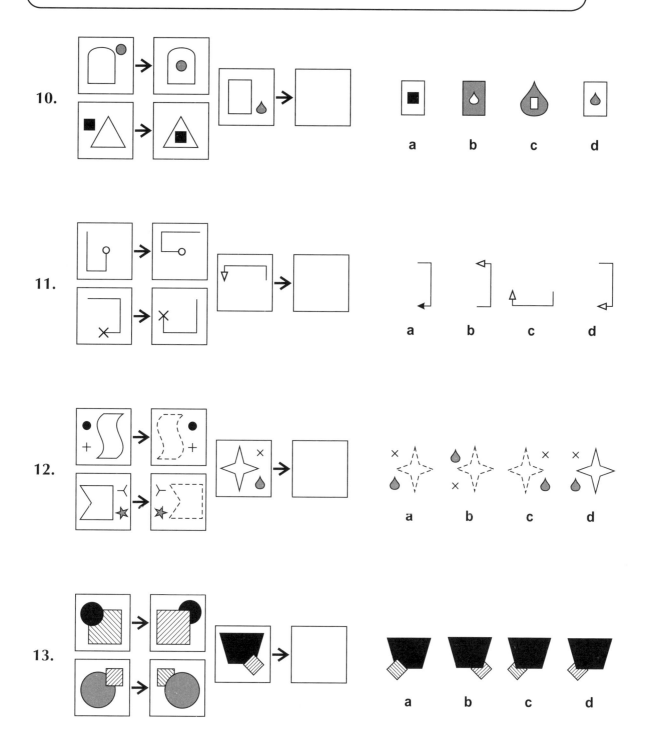

10.

a   b   c   d

11.

a   b   c   d

12.

a   b   c   d

13.

a   b   c   d

Work out which of the options best fits in place of the missing square in the series.

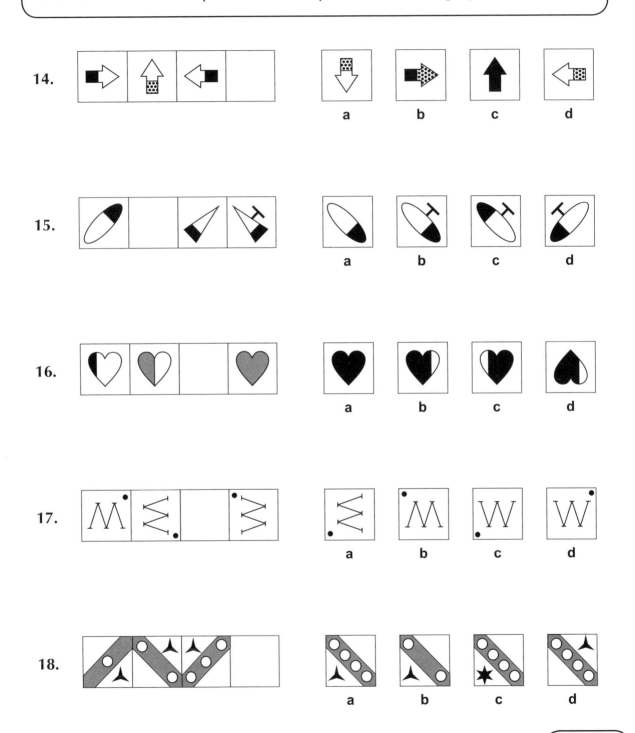

14.

15.

16.

17.

18.

a   b   c   d

/ 18

Test 30

You have **10 minutes** to do this test. Circle the letter for each correct answer.

Work out which option is most like the two figures on the left.

1. |

                    a   **b**   **c**   **d**

2. |

                    a   **b**   **c**   **d**

3. |

                    a   **b**   **c**   **d**

4. |

                    a   **b**   **c**   **d**

5. |

                    a   **b**   **c**   **d**

Work out which of the options best fits in place of the missing square in the grid.

6.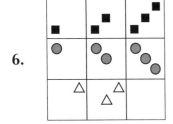

a   b   c   d   e

7.

a   b   c   d   e

8.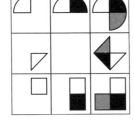

a   b   c   d   e

9.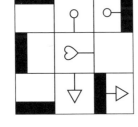

a   b   c   d   e

Work out which option would look like the figure on the left if it was reflected over the line.

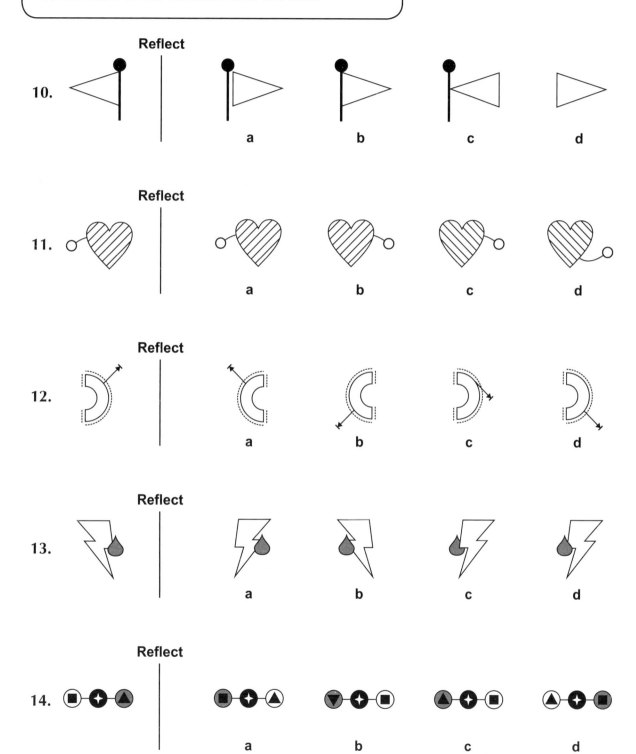

10.   **Reflect**

    a   b   c   d

11.   **Reflect**

    a   b   c   d

12.   **Reflect**

    a   b   c   d

13.   **Reflect**

    a   b   c   d

14.   **Reflect**

    a   b   c   d

135

Work out which set of blocks can be put together to make the 3D figure on the left.

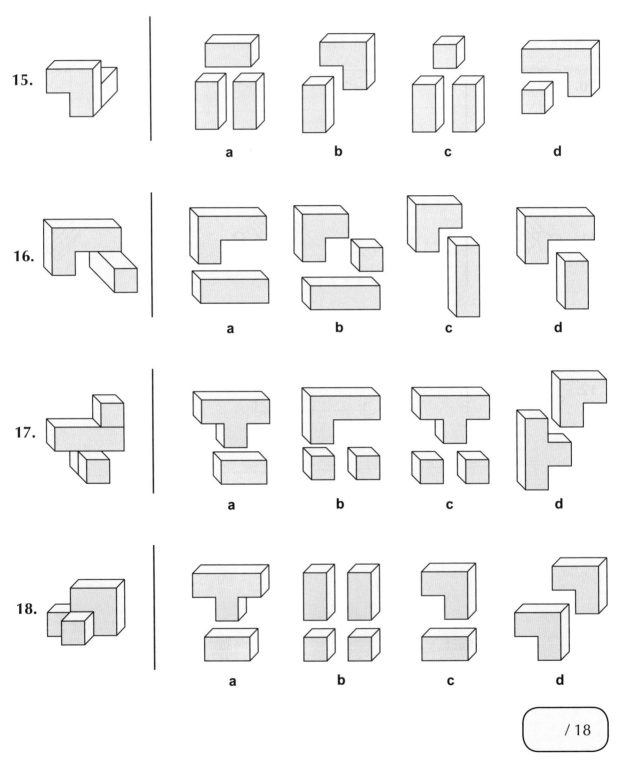

15.

a   b   c   d

16.

a   b   c   d

17.

a   b   c   d

18.

a   b   c   d

/ 18

You have **10 minutes** to do this test. Circle the letter for each correct answer.

Work out which 3D figure in the grey box has been rotated to make the new 3D figure.

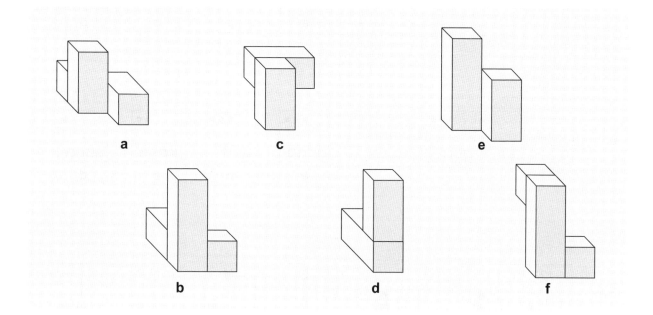

a

c

e

b

d

f

1.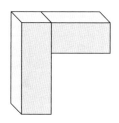

a   d

b   e

c   f

2.

a   d

b   e

c   f

3.

a   d

b   e

c   f

4.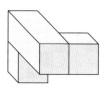

a   d

b   e

c   f

137

Work out which of the options best fits in place of the missing square in the series.

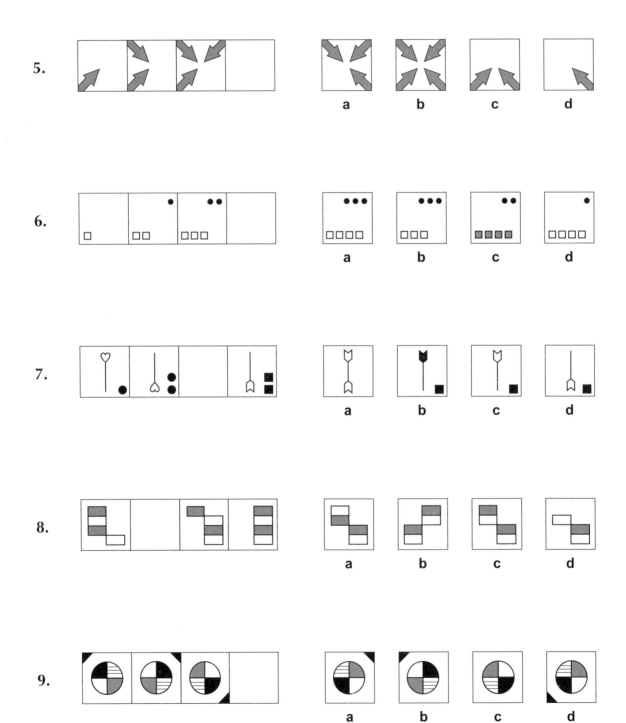

5.   a   b   c   d

6.   a   b   c   d

7.   a   b   c   d

8.   a   b   c   d

9.   a   b   c   d

Work out which of the options best fits in place of the missing hexagon in the grid.

10.

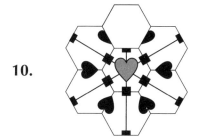

 a

 b

 c

 d

11.

 a

 b

 c

 d

12.

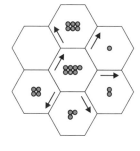

 a

 b

 c

 d

13.

 a

 b

 c

d

Test 31

Find the figure in each row that is most unlike the others.

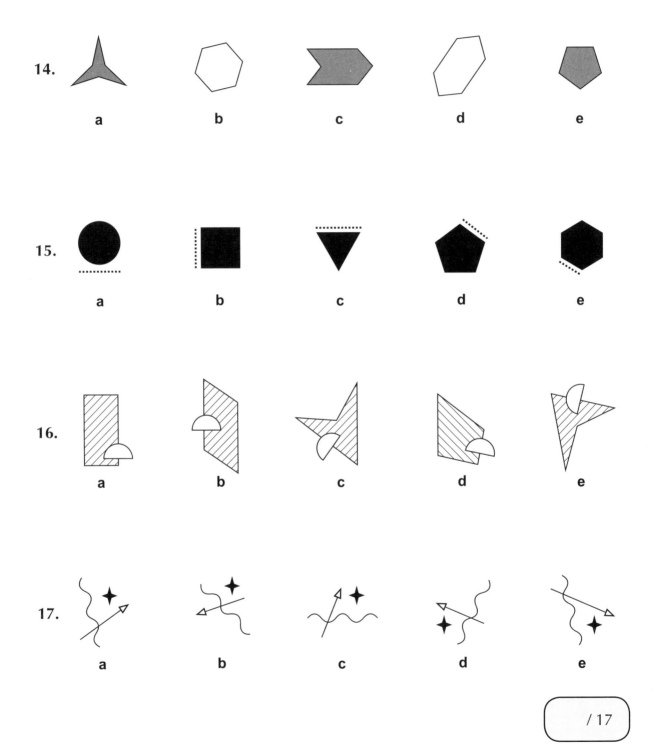

14.

a   b   c   d   e

15.

a   b   c   d   e

16.

a   b   c   d   e

17.

a   b   c   d   e

/ 17

Give these puzzles a go! They're a great way to practise some of the skills you'll need.

The Last Piece of the Puzzle

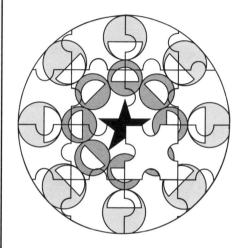

Cyril is finishing his jigsaw puzzle, as shown on the left. But he's missing the last piece.

What does the missing piece look like? Circle your answer.

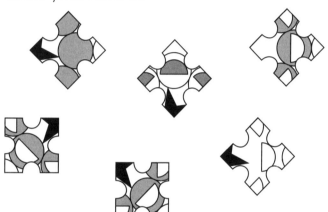

Flood Warning!

It has been raining continuously for a week. Adam wants to stop his house flooding, so he builds a flood defence in front, as shown below.

Complete Adam's map to show what his house and flood defence would look like from the air.

Adam's House

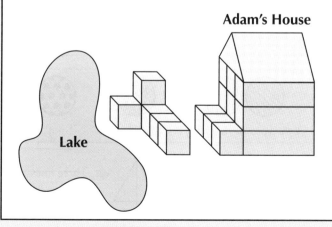

Lake

Map

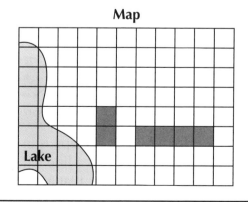

Lake

141

Glossary

Rotation and Reflection

Rotation is when a shape is turned clockwise or anticlockwise from its starting point.

Example shape

90 degree clockwise rotation

45 degree anticlockwise rotation

180 degree rotation

Reflection is when something is mirrored over an imaginary line.

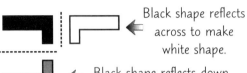

Black shape reflects across to make white shape.

Black shape reflects down to make grey shape.

3D Rotation

There are **three planes** that a 3D shape can be rotated in.

1. 90 degrees towards you, top-to-bottom

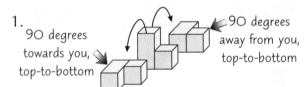

90 degrees away from you, top-to-bottom

2.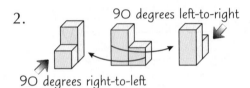

90 degrees left-to-right

90 degrees right-to-left

3. 90 degrees anticlockwise in the plane of the page

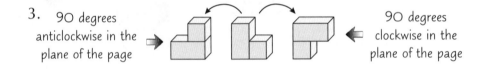

90 degrees clockwise in the plane of the page

Other Terms

Figure — the picture as a whole that makes up one example or option in a question.

Arrow-style Line — a line with a small shape at one end.

Line Types:

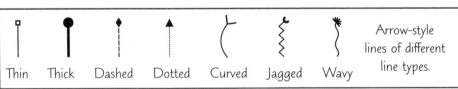

Thin   Thick   Dashed   Dotted   Curved   Jagged   Wavy

Arrow-style lines of different line types.

Shading Types:

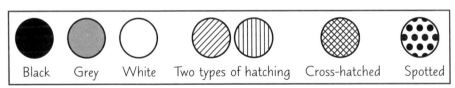

Black   Grey   White   Two types of hatching   Cross-hatched   Spotted

Layering — when a shape is in front of or behind other shapes.

Line of Symmetry — a line which splits a shape into halves that are reflections of each other.

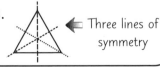

Three lines of symmetry

N5XPDF1